Hawkins\Brown

Hawkins\Brown
It's Your Building

MERRELL
LONDON · NEW YORK

Contents

Hugh Pearman

There are architects who make a lot of noise about what they do, and there are architects, like Hawkins\Brown, who just get on and do it. Not that anyone ever accused Roger Hawkins and Russell Brown, the men at the helm of the practice they founded thirty years ago, of being averse to publicity. They produce buildings that are distinctive and rich in ideas, regulars on the awards circuit. They operate across several important sectors, including universities – Russell Group, plus Oxford at the top of the pile. They are innovators in housing and transport. They make it their business to be visible and engaged. They make sure their work is recorded and published – hence this book. They wear distinctive shirts, they do not shy away from colour and decoration, they love working with artists, they like to project a slightly alternative image. They are, to shudderingly flog a malnourished word, 'creatives'. But they might also be regarded as extreme pragmatists, strategists and long-termists. They see architecture as just one very significant part of making a better built environment. They know that clever concept stuff must be followed through properly, and they know that that in turn calls for skill and organization and like-minded friends in the industry.

The date they founded their practice is important. In 1988, when Hawkins and Brown quit their jobs at the well-regarded practice Rock Townsend to set up in business together, the Lawson Boom was at its height. The economy was as frothy as the commercial postmodernism then current, which meant that the fledgling Hawkins\Brown had the recession of the early 1990s to negotiate. Getting through that toughened them up nicely: nothing was handed to them on a plate. It taught them not to depend too heavily on any one sector, but to be generalists, active in many fields at once. Apart from making business sense, this also allows the cross-fertilization of ideas between building types: to combine flats and a school in one efficient, compact building, for instance.

The practice that began with some low-key but imaginative east London community projects has grown to be a considerable powerhouse in the profession, employing some 270 people at the time of writing. It has a separate office in Manchester, Studio North. It has overseas projects under its belt and an outpost in California. It is on its way to becoming an employee-owned enterprise, and is close to having a 50:50 gender balance. So how did they get from 1988 to here, and, just as importantly, how do they retain the freshness of an originally personality-driven practice that – with its twenty-three other partners sharing in the ownership of the business – is now more of a collaborative venture?

Hawkins and Brown had to learn the art of the pitch, and they had to have a plan. Their initial idea was to do half of their work in the private sector – commerce – and half in the public sector – including schools and universities, but also public transport. The latter started with London Underground projects. That means infrastructure, hence the practice's long, long association with Crossrail, or the Elizabeth line, as this first London express metro is called in use, along with continuing, ever more complex work for Transport for London. Designing and delivering public infrastructure means working in an engineering-led team, often alongside other architects. There is not much place for the aesthetic fainting-couch there, but there is plenty of room for determination, even obstinacy, when it comes to seeing your ideas through to reality.

The Tottenham Court Road Tube/Crossrail interchange, with its restored Eduardo Paolozzi mosaics and new permanent artwork by Daniel Buren and others, is testament as much to doggedness as to flair; were it not for the architects' insistence, there would have been considerably greater loss of Paolozzi's 1970s work. Hawkins\Brown championed the art, old and new, while dealing with the incredibly complex physical and logistical problems of the site. This runs from Charing Cross Road beneath Soho Square to Dean Street and Great Chapel Street in Soho, and they saw its two ends in terms of 'day' and 'night', an approach that comes through in the interiors. Interior design has always been a strong point for Hawkins\Brown – something that is well worth noting, since by no means all practices are good at it. Theirs is a different sensibility, adding detail and richness at the point of design rather than as a later add-on, often done by others.

Also typically of Hawkins\Brown's approach, they looked at the whole complex business of designing for infrastructure and decided that the smart thing to do was to get into what is known as the 'delivery side'. These days, architecture is increasingly a two-stage process – design and delivery – and it is by no means always the case that the same architect will do both, or even want to do both. As an architect one can regret this, or one can accept it, engage with it and see what can be brought to the party. So while the practice both designed and delivered its Tottenham Court Road Crossrail station (in reality two stations, at Charing Cross Road and Dean

The Architecture of Ingenuity

Street, or three if you add the Underground), it also worked on the delivery side at Bond Street (concept design by John McAslan + Partners) and Liverpool Street (WilkinsonEyre). That's OK: credit where it's due is the mantra.

An earlier Hawkins\Brown book was themed on the idea of collaboration, a key example being the firm's work with Studio Egret West on the radical reinvention of the listed Park Hill council estate in Sheffield for the developer Urban Splash, under the eye of what was then English Heritage. To this day, I'm not wholly sure exactly who did what there. Does that matter? Does the public care? No, it does not. Passers-by never knew the name of the original tweed-and-pipes architects of Park Hill, and – despite the fact that the transformed complex was shortlisted for the Stirling Prize – they won't know who did the upgrade. Nor will all but the minutest fraction of the millions who use the Elizabeth line have a clue. They'll just, probably subconsciously, appreciate the environment.

It's important not to get precious about this. In 95 per cent of all architecture, good work is its own reward. Those who need to know, know. Brown says of the young architects who first designed Park Hill in the late 1950s (Ivor Smith and Jack Lynn, then working for Sheffield City Council): 'They had the confidence that they could make a difference – I really like that attitude.' Similarly Hawkins and Brown, as rookie architects at Rock Townsend, were given responsibility for large projects early. This attitude is passed on in their own practice, where younger colleagues are given their heads if they come up with strong ideas. In this way the rotated X-plan cross-laminated timber housing block of Wenlock Basin came to be, for instance:

a rare example of a genuinely innovative and different-looking building emerging in the east London housing boom. Confidence is key. When it comes to housing, for instance – of all tenures – there is no need to reinvent the wheel, says Brown, but there are small, significant moves you can make, internally and externally, that enrich the experience of living, give a sense of arrival and safety, command views and silently make encounters with neighbours a natural thing.

Highly significant for the practice in the alternative housing sector is East Village in Stratford, east London. It is cross-fertilization again: learning from both the social streets-in-the-sky of Park Hill and the use of strong and varied colour as practised at Oxford University (of which more below). It's an 'anti-beige, pro-neighbour' project, nudging its inhabitants towards community-mindedness through design, incorporating shops, businesses, leisure and distinctive landscape. So different from the Eastern European feel of the former Athlete's Village blocks here, it should be an exemplar in the build-to-rent market. It demonstrates that all housing blocks do not have to embody the same formulaic response.

When it comes to the career trajectory of the practice's founders, it may be relevant that they started off outside the London architectural echo chamber. Neither is from London originally (both grew up in Nottingham, not that they knew each other back then). Neither studied architecture in London, preferring other good schools. They met, it is true, working at a London practice, and they set up their business in the capital, and thrived. But I wonder if they went native. I wonder if there isn't, lurking in there somewhere, the merest touch of the

psychology of the incomer. There is also a sense of humanism, of contextual modernism; the likes of Ralph Erskine, Herman Hertzberger and Aldo van Eyck – all from the 'alternative tradition' of modernism – tend to crop up in conversation rather more than hardliners such as Le Corbusier and Ludwig Mies van der Rohe, for example. The determination not to have a signature style opens up the design possibilities considerably. That is then communicated by example to the successive generations of architects who have come into the expanding practice, with its studios of about twenty-five people each, from all over the world. Perhaps – especially given the practice has weathered two serious economic recessions – it boils down to this: everything's an opportunity, so take it.

Such an approach could lead to a breakout trophy building such as the University of Oxford's New Biochemistry Building (2008), which celebrates the activities within and – very characteristic of the practice – dares to be free with colour. Rethinking the building type from first principles, reversing the usual laboratory building layout by making the labs visible on the outside while encouraging interaction at the centre of the plan, was a key moment. The project introduced the firm to a new kind of demanding, high-profile client who, along with the rest of the project team, stayed loyal, moving on to a further phase and the separate Beecroft Building.

Later came a lion's-den moment: to rebuild the Bartlett School of Architecture at University College London. The Bartlett and many of its alumni are world-famous, yet this was to be a refurbishment of a nondescript 1960s building. Refurb is sometimes seen as a second-class option, but for no reason. Making better use of existing structures is a faster, more energy-conscious way to proceed, and retains traces of history. Today the building looks new from the outside, but inside it shows off its construction in a subtly didactic way.

More radical still is Here East, where the enormous dumb metal sheds of the Media Centre bequeathed by the London 2012 Olympics have become a high-tech village modelled on neighbouring Hackney Wick, with its adapted industrial buildings. Walk up the River Lea towpath there and you encounter just one part of this thinking, a waterside street of cafe and restaurant culture that immediately civilizes what was previously just a fenced-off blank wall. There's more than one way to do good stuff, so imagine how that might happen, don't give up – and enjoy yourself while you're about it.

All hardworking architecture practices become almost monastic communities, not in the ascetic sense, but in the sense of self-reliance, common purpose, being part of a family. I like visiting architects' offices to compare and contrast how they manage this. The Hawkins\Brown office in a former lift factory in Clerkenwell has some pleasingly eccentric touches when it comes, say, to the domestic-influenced interior design of the meeting rooms, or the flashes of colour in the window reveals. The two founders set great store by the social aspect of their firm. Weddings between staff members are commonplace, it seems. Over the years I have also noticed a number of top-notch draughtspeople in the practice; if you run an annual architectural drawing competition, as I do at the *RIBA Journal*, you learn where such talent lies. It turns out this is encouraged. Drawings are displayed for their own sake along with all the

working-drawing paraphernalia of the practice. There are life-drawing and watercolour classes. Everyone is given free membership of the nearby Barbican arts complex, and there are office study trips to agreeable overseas locations where there just happen to be best-practice buildings to learn from. Some of the presentation drawings and models in the office have a pleasing touch of student enthusiasm about them, revelling in the tactility of the object alongside the information conveyed. And then there's the special place.

Russell Brown took me there. It's an annex – which is common enough when a practice outgrows its premises. In this case, though, it's a hushed environment, devoted to competitions and the early stages of commissioned projects, furnished with mid-twentieth-century furniture. It's a different kind of Clerkenwell industrial building, more watchmaker than printer, you might say, except that its most recent use was as a photographer's studio. The idea is to have a place that is literally and metaphorically apart from the distractions of the more hectic main office; a place in which to work in a more concentrated fashion. The analogue way of doing things exists alongside the digital: tracing paper is sometimes laid over computer screens, felt-tip pens produced. It's not hard to see that, when a creative business gets big, this is one way of returning to the approach that brought that success in the first place.

Planning and subsequently orchestrating the direction of an architecture practice is fine in principle, but less easy to achieve in today's conditions, which tend to push architects towards specialization. Some seem to live and breathe the rarefied air of art galleries, others are immersed in the greasepaint of the theatre world,

more become the go-to people for hospitals or social housing or tricky conservation projects, and yet more feed the insatiable demand for speculative commercial floorspace. There's no reason at all not to take this route – all ways of doing architecture are permissible – but it can narrow down the range of possible responses. While there is plenty to question in the way architectural competitions and selection processes operate, at least they tend to cast the net rather wider, allowing firms other than the usual suspects to get a look-in. Hawkins\Brown have succeeded in not being typecast, and doing well in competitions. Call it general practice if you will, or multi-specialism if you must. Obviously, the projects in this book are carefully selected to show the breadth of the practice's work, but then again, the breadth of work is there to show.

Let's take two. It's hard to believe that the same practice has produced, over many years, the new concept of a civic centre called the Corby Cube and the sequence of riparian interventions down the River Thames through London associated with the Thames Tideway Tunnel. But the common thread is a desire to question accepted responses. In the case of the Corby Cube, the idea was to combine what had originally been earmarked as two buildings – theatre/cultural centre and town hall/library – into one Platonic object, the Cube. Another bringing-together of typologies. Achieving this building satisfactorily turned out to be an eleven-year saga. Hawkins\Brown themselves might be forgiven for not wanting to revisit what became a controversial and protracted project, but not a bit of it: they are fiercely proud of the Cube and of the way the power of the idea finally won through, thanks to their typical persistence. It certainly helps that the place has proved very popular with the public. As a consequence, the broad-striped cubic form with its complex interlocking spaces is becoming a symbol of the revival of this post-industrial Northamptonshire town.

With the Thames Tideway Tunnel, the firm's interest in infrastructure surfaces again. Most people don't even know that the tunnel is happening, or if they do, they dismiss it as just another disruptive bit of engineering that – unlike Crossrail, with its surface sproutings – will be invisible. The Tideway Tunnel is a super-sewer running through the centre of London. It will bring massive environmental improvement to the Thames by hugely increasing the capacity of the overloaded Victorian sewerage system originally designed and built by Sir Joseph Bazalgette (who in the process created the Thames Embankment).

What have architects got to do with all that? This: at intervals along the banks of the Thames, sometimes in very prominent locations, there will be sunken pumping stations and shafts allowing access to the subterranean world. This gives the opportunity to do interesting things on the riverbanks as the roofs of these otherwise mute objects become part of the ground condition. Six will become landscaped, terraced or stepped, interventions in the progress of the river; they will be differently shaped for different functions, and because of the hydrology of the (by then sparklingly clean) tideway. We'll be able to enjoy the tidal river in a new way, up (or down) close. Different artists are working with the architects to define the character of each public space.

This kind of work is hard to categorize. It's not really an architectural typology, but it's more than landscape – more a kind of orchestrated happenstance. But for that reason there are no preconceptions. The Tideway Tunnel is happening, and therefore, with all due persistence, so will these unusual new public areas, redefining our relationship with the river. What a great sequence of spaces to be asked to design.

One word that springs to mind when looking through the projects in this book is 'range'. If the stripy Corby Cube or the colour-washed conjoined housing towers of Stratford's East Village represent one vigorous approach and two refreshed typologies, and Here East an exuberant reworking on a huge scale, then what does one make of the careful extension of a Victorian warehouse in Southwark's Great Suffolk Street, that long, curving canyon of railway arches that helps to define the character of post-industrial inner London? This job is in a way a cloning exercise, taking the external architecture of an existing building and reproducing it – complete with raw industrial interior finishes – alongside. Together with an extra floor on top, this is an exercise in maximizing lettable floor area, of course, but also a way to acknowledge and densify the character of the area. Restraint is the watchword, along with a richness of good exposed materials, including bespoke brick. Plasterboard is banned.

The founding partners of Hawkins\Brown are justly proud of their awards record, as a practice, as well as for individual buildings. It reflects their culture as a good place in which to work, as well as their approach to design and the business of design. That's important. So is leading the thinking on the increasing complexity of buildings, not just technically, but also functionally. We are in the era of mixed-use architecture on a grand scale, and that is tremendous for the vitality of our towns and cities.

And then one looks at the emerging facades of the practice's Beecroft Building on the Parks edge of the University of Oxford, next to Keble College, and the word that comes to mind is 'ingenuity'. In a city like this, what is context, and how can one fit in with that? The challenge is to introduce a large, highly serviced laboratory building – much of it below ground, but with plenty above as well – in such a way as to suggest effortless quality and that hard-to-define Oxford-ness. The ghost of Ruskin (who hated Keble, which is now listed Grade I) hovers over such endeavours.

Confidence wins through once more. Take a look, and you'll see what I mean. It's not easy to create a building like that, in such a place. That tells you a lot about the nature of the architects who bring it into being. Practicality, aesthetics and a strong dash of joie-de-vivre, all served in what, after all, is a classic definition of the nature of architecture. To get to this point in so many areas of work requires more than just confidence, however. It is clear that there is a very strong knowledge base. Hawkins\Brown know what works and, more intriguingly, they know what *will* work – even if it has never been done before.

The Bartlett School of Architecture at University College London (UCL) was struggling to cram more students into Wates House at 22 Gordon Street, the school's fortress-like home in Bloomsbury since the 1970s. This project, one of a number undertaken by Hawkins\Brown as part of the wider 'Transforming UCL' programme, is a 'deep retrofit' that retains the structural concrete frame while making bold interventions to create a radical new building that has doubled teaching and research space.

Back to the drawing board

The Bartlett School of Architecture is internationally acclaimed for its innovative research and teaching, and has a reputation for nurturing the best of the best. But with 850 students crammed into space that was originally designed to accommodate just 90 staff and 380 students, Wates House was fit to burst.

For architects, there is probably no more daunting task than to design a building for architecture students. As well as exercising every bit of knowledge they had about the school, Hawkins\Brown went deeper, returning to first principles to interrogate the brief in order to create a truly viable future for the new building. The team spent two years working with the school to improve their understanding of the existing structure's flaws and successes. Eventually, it was decided that a sticking-plaster refurbishment consisting of replacing windows and adding a modest extension was not going to be enough. Something more radical, more in tune with the spirit of the school itself, was called for.

When work got under way, the School of Architecture was moved temporarily to converted warehouses on Hampstead Road, a project also carried out by Hawkins\Brown. The open-plan set-up there proved to be a fertile testing ground for the students of the school.

Deep retrofit

The building has been stripped back to its concrete frame and cores. Columns have been strengthened and new steelwork put in place, and a fifth and sixth floor have been added, as well as a full-height extension to the south. A 1.5-metre plywood-lined perimeter extension adds even more space while bringing the facade up to the property boundary, so that the building fills the site snugly above ground.

Retaining the building not only saved precious memories but also resulted in a faster programme and a smaller price tag; the project was £10m cheaper than a full demolition and rebuild. Add to that the 440 tonnes of carbon saved by retaining the original concrete structure and it's hard to doubt that the client made the right decision.

This part of Bloomsbury has a mixture of buildings in varying scales, many of them listed. Every turn of the head reveals another style – Brutalist, Modernist, Georgian, Neoclassical. The school had to respond positively to this mishmash of historic buildings, and so it does. Wrapped in a skin of handmade waterstruck bricks with repetitive window frames and reveals lined in anodized aluminium, the coherent facade respects the proportions of the surrounding architecture.

Creative collisions

Everything has been designed with collaboration and adaptation in mind. Rather than coming through the building and jumping straight into the lift, people are drawn to the new dark-steel staircase. Conceived as 'a social

Opposite The accessible school of architecture has transformed Wates House, creating a new identity for a new generation of designers.

Right A staircase inserted into the heart of the building makes new connections and social spaces.

The Bartlett School of Architecture

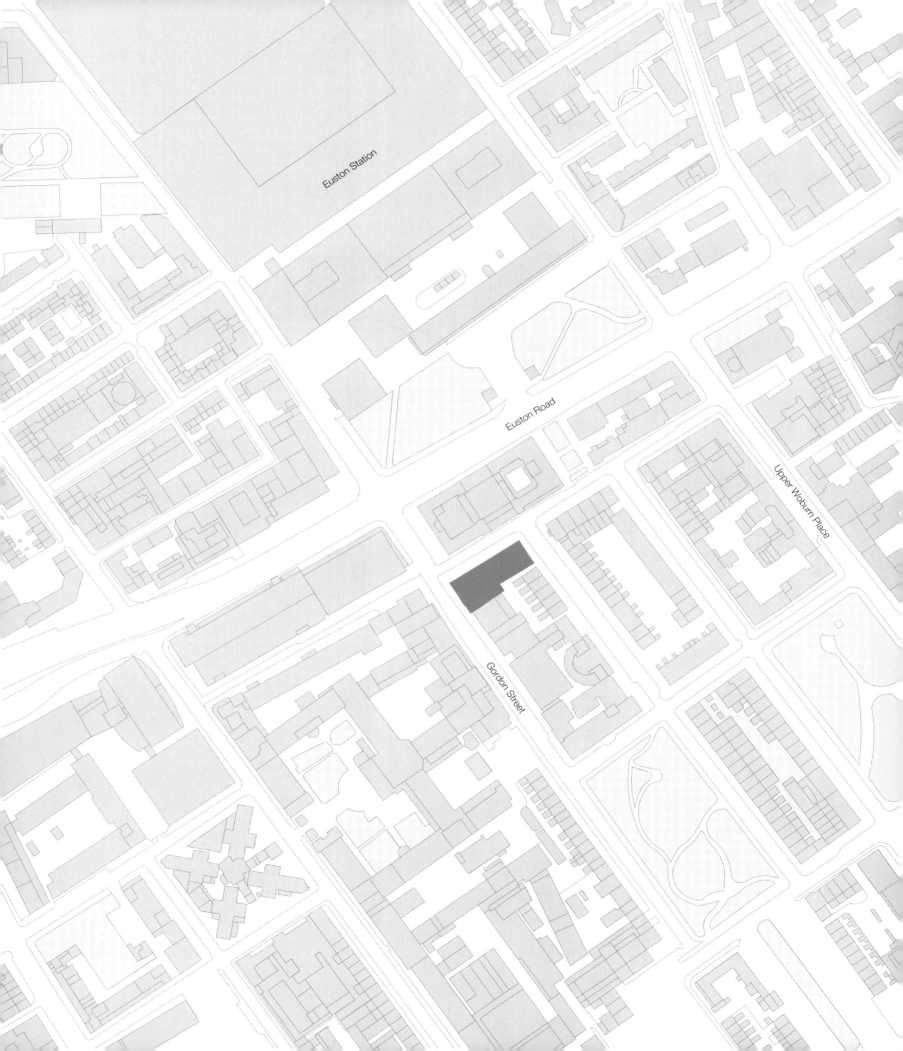

Euston Station

Euston Road

Upper Woburn Place

Gordon Street

generator', it is slotted into a full-height atrium in the new side extension and cuts its way through the plan, connecting all levels both physically and visually while encouraging movement and interaction.

Internally, the building has been reconfigured to create more space, doubling the useable area available to the school. The faculty library and fourth-floor School of Planning have moved into another building, freeing much-needed space for the architecture department's 850 students. Studio space is open-plan, naturally lit and supported by large areas that are ripe for experimentation, testing and play. Deliberately pared-down, these areas are neutral and hardwearing with concrete floors and white walls, ready to become whatever they need to be.

The interplay of old and new has been delicately handled. Wates House is ever-present, and its exposed frame contrasts with the plywood of the new extension, a material that is carried through into the sliding doors and moveable walls. Floor-to-ceiling windows open up long views across the nearby rooftops, connecting students and staff with this dense and historic part of the city, and the city with the school.

The new building has turned to face the city and thrown open its doors, with a ground floor dedicated to a cafe and exhibition space that promote the discussion of, and engagement with, architecture. A shop window animates the building with a new double-height entrance space that enhances the connection to the street.

Coming home

Ultimately, the Bartlett needed more space: no bells and whistles, just space. And that's what it now has, space in a building that enhances the lives of the students and academics who use it every day, as well as visitors and the city itself. Remarkably, the year 2017 was the first time the Bartlett's Summer Show had been held in the school building for sixteen years; there just wasn't room before. But, as thousands of visitors wove their way through the renewed building, making links with studio and exhibition spaces, it felt as though the Bartlett had finally come home.

22 Gordon Street now sits assuredly in its conservation area setting, while retaining the spirit of the 1970s building.

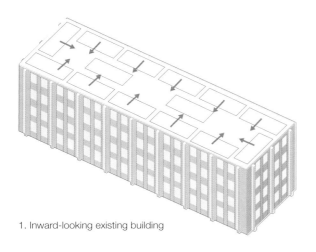

1. Inward-looking existing building

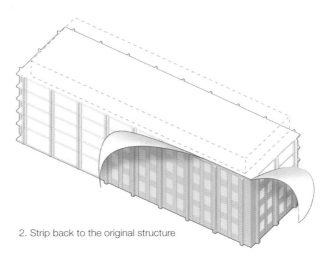

Deep retrofit: Hawkins\Brown undertook a careful balance of new-build and refurbishment to adapt, reconfigure and extend the original building.

2. Strip back to the original structure

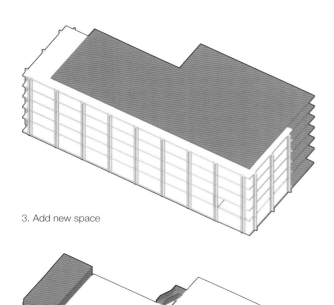

3. Add new space

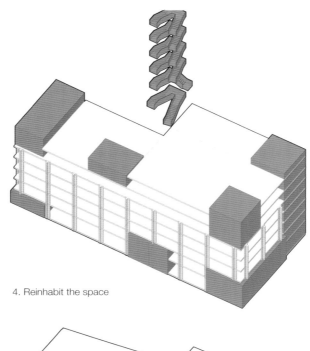

4. Reinhabit the space

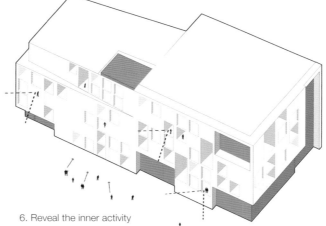

5. Add a flexible inner skin

6. Reveal the inner activity

The school was stripped back
to its reinforced-concrete frame,
enabling major interventions to
the structure.

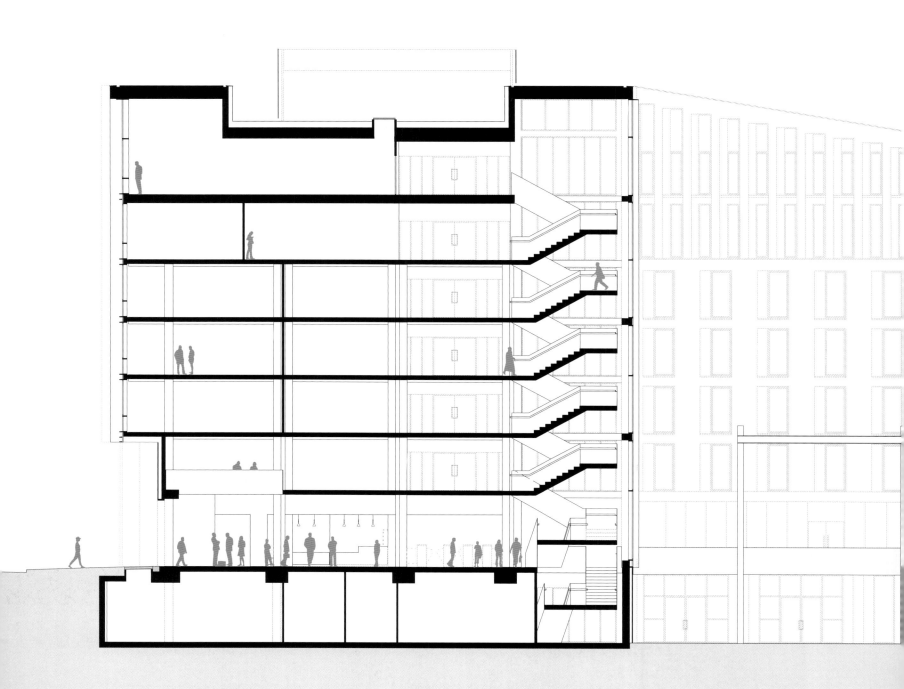

PROJECT DATA

LOCATION
Bloomsbury, London

CLIENT
University College London

SIZE
9,000 square metres

START DATE
2012

COMPLETION DATE
2016

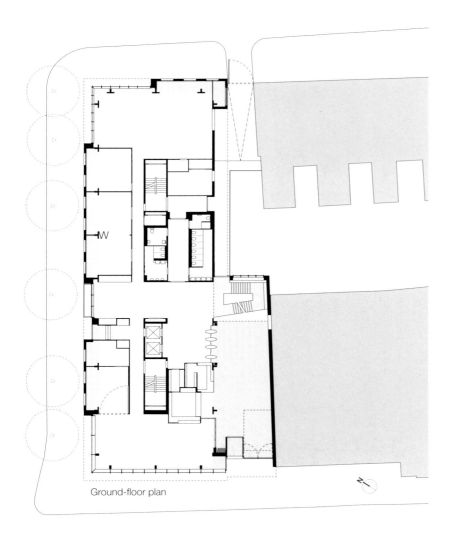

Ground-floor plan

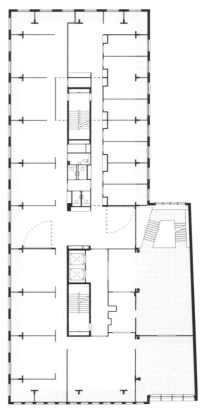

Upper-floor plan

Opposite Section through the full-height extension and new staircase.

Above The ground-floor plan shows the new skin wrapping around the original structure.

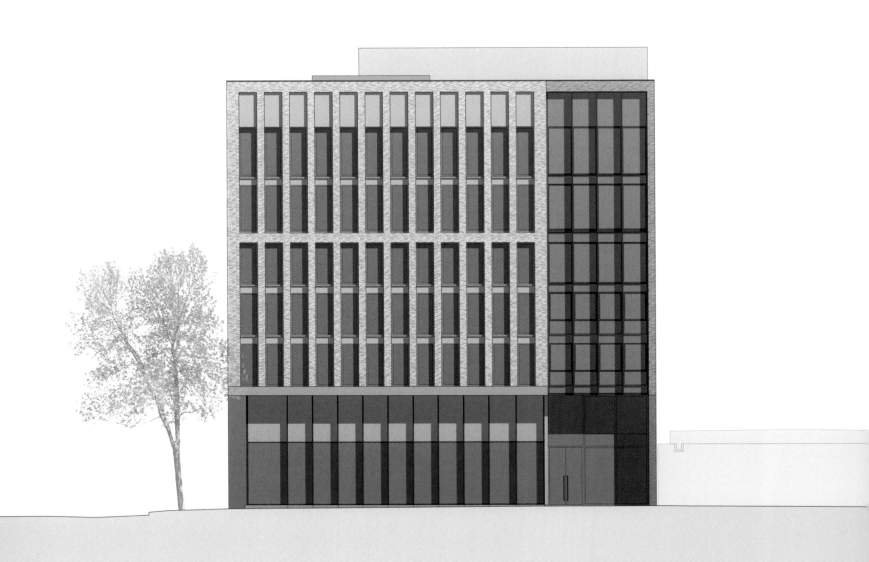

22 Gordon Street introduces a new generation of staff and students to the possibility of what can happen through effective collaboration.

ALAN PENN, DEAN OF THE BARTLETT,
UCL FACULTY OF THE BUILT ENVIRONMENT

Opposite West elevation.

Right Model. The building is on a constrained site in a conservation area, but through careful dialogue Hawkins\Brown have created a contemporary building that is sensitive to its context.

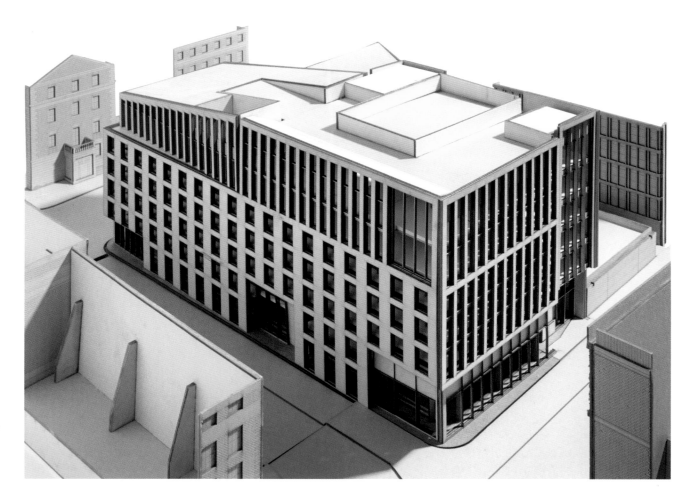

Exposed original columns and detailing indicate the transition into the new plywood-lined extension of studio space with bespoke joinery and large picture windows.

The flexible ground-floor space can be used in various ways, and maximizes views into and out of the building.

Overleaf The newly transformed building photographed shortly after its opening in 2017.

Corby Cube, a landmark glazed box in the very centre of the new urban quarter of this East Midlands town, is more than an emblem of civic pride – it's a destination. Open day and night, it forms the centrepiece of Corby's radical regeneration, creating connections across the town while housing a host of civic, cultural and community functions. The bold ambition at its heart – to combine civic and arts functions in one building – has led the way in local authorities streamlining their services not only to benefit their communities, but also to get more bang for their buck.

Boom town

The influx of thousands of Scots steelworkers to the Stewarts & Lloyds works in the 1930s transformed Corby from a village of 1,500 people into a thriving industrial town. But by the 1980s the town's fortunes were waning. When the steelworks closed, in December 1980, many believed Corby's heart had been ripped out. Looking back at the town's rapid decline, it is hard not to agree, but Corby has come a long way since then. Concerted investment in the town's regeneration strategy, driven by North Northants Development Company, has led to a new era for the town that was once dubbed 'Little Scotland'. Just over an hour by rail from London St Pancras station, it is now one of the

best-connected parts of the country and has one of the fastest-growing populations.

Two-in-one

In 2004 an international design competition was launched for a new town hall and arts centre in Corby. The two new buildings were intended to be the gateway to the town's regeneration strategy, and to help revitalize Corby as a vibrant place in which to live, work, visit and do business.

Hawkins\Brown won the competition, beating the big hitters of the day to gain one of their most prestigious jobs to date. Although designed during the boom of the early 2000s, the Cube was built at a time of spending reviews and huge funding cuts, so the central tenet of the architects' plan – combining the two buildings into one – was a bold response that paid off. Not only did the proposal provide benefits by bringing people together and creating a central hub, but also it realized massive savings in capital and running costs by sharing facilities and infrastructure. It also freed up the second proposed site for other redevelopment.

Box of tricks

The building packs in all the functions of the two original briefs. That is no mean feat, considering the variety of spaces required: a 445-seat theatre, flexible studios, a box office, a public library, a cafe, a one-stop shop, a register office and a council chamber, as well as various gathering areas.

In a building where so much is going on, it can be difficult to get people to where they need to go, but the Cube manages this very successfully. The library ramp acts as an extension of the public realm, wrapping around the building and drawing people up and through. An internal street of sorts, it forms the Cube's main circulation. It inclines up to the one-stop shop, where the thoroughfare continues as a linear stair, culminating in a helical staircase that connects the civic offices and council chambers to a rooftop garden. As you work your way up the building, the character of the spaces becomes more intimate, as befits the civic functions on the upper levels. It's a wonderful meander, rather than a dull trudge, animated with spaces designed for interaction and engagement. The interior design helps to define the various areas, distinguishing subtly between the formal and informal, the communal and the more intimate.

The Cube is contemporary through and through, with concrete walls and soffits that are accented with vibrant flashes of colour and bold graphics. The library, a far cry from the stuffy, dusty rooms of the past, buzzes with life

The popular theatre, which was the first in the UK to be awarded a BREEAM Excellent rating, incorporates innovative technology including curved retractable seating and a moveable proscenium.

Corby Cube

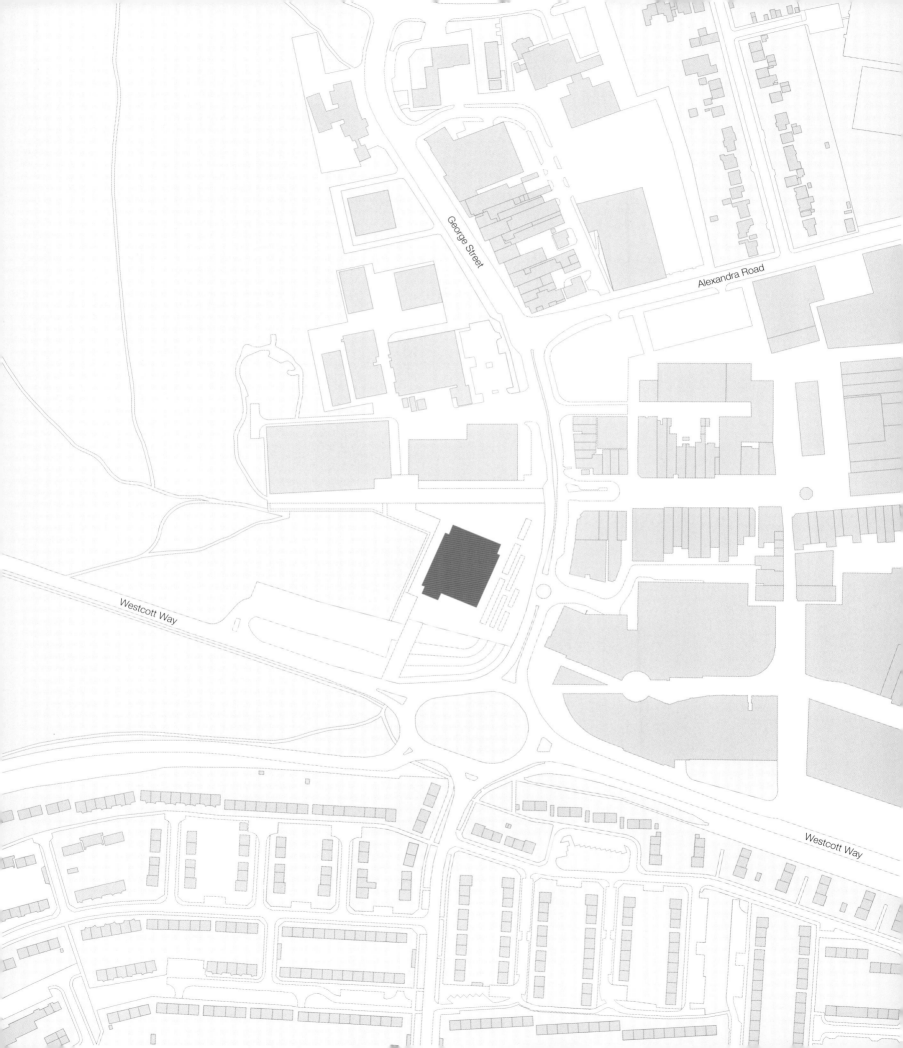

and activity. Its bright, welcoming spaces are full of people borrowing books, chatting or waiting for an appointment upstairs. It is easy to see why there has been a 50 per cent increase in library membership since its services were moved to the Cube.

The building's striking glazed facade reflects the town, while inviting you to look inside. Made up of six types of glass, the banding of the facade responds to the orientation of the internal spaces. The ratio of solid to void gradually expands and contracts on all four elevations, and it not only looks good, but is also working hard to perform well in environmental terms. The alternating glass banding means that daylight is maximized in the library, council chamber and offices, but solar gain is prevented elsewhere.

The Cube's 445-seat community theatre, known as the Core, might be sunk underground, but it's the heart of the building. The interior design takes its cue from traditional theatres such as the Old Vic and the Royal Court in London, with walnut and plush fabrics that create a glamorous, intimate space for theatre and music. A curved, retractable seating system (the first of its kind in the United Kingdom at the time) and moveable proscenium arch mean that the theatre is flexible enough to host a diverse programme of events.

Hawkins\Brown took a risk in challenging the original brief, but Corby enjoys the reward. By listening to the local community and understanding their varied needs and desires, the architects have created a truly sustainable building. Not only is the Cube rated BREEAM Excellent, but also it's full of people day and night, and nothing makes a building more sustainable than when it is well-used and well-loved.

Right Hawkins\Brown's competition-winning model reveals the practice's ambitious vision to combine civic and arts functions in one lively twenty-four-hour hub.

Far right The various uses within Corby Cube fit into a compact square plan around a central core.

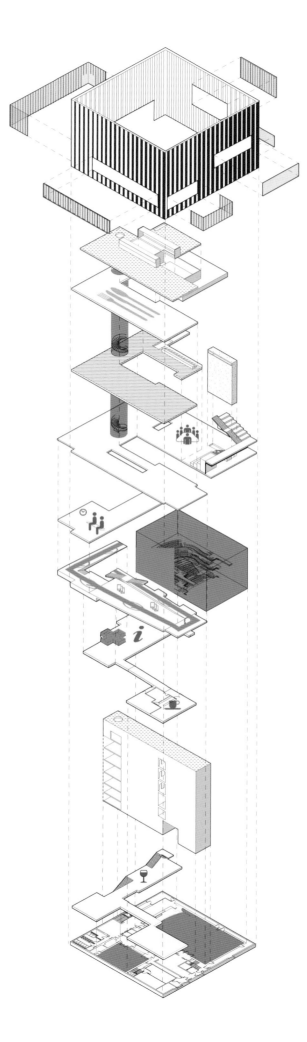

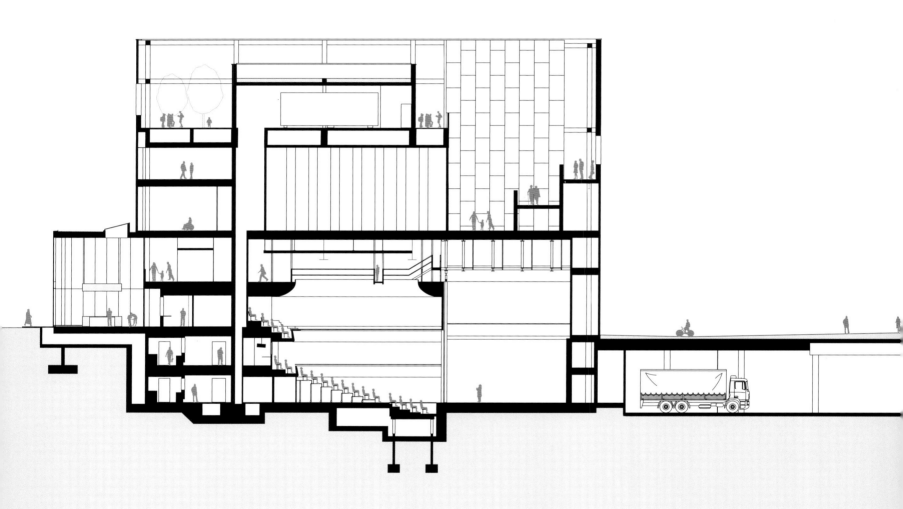

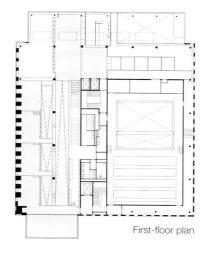

First-floor plan

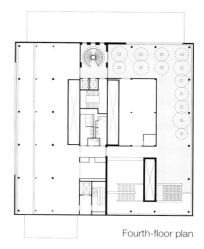

Fourth-floor plan

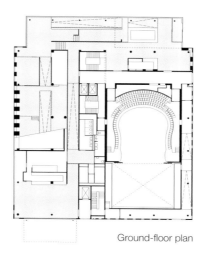

Ground-floor plan

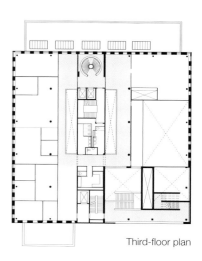

Third-floor plan

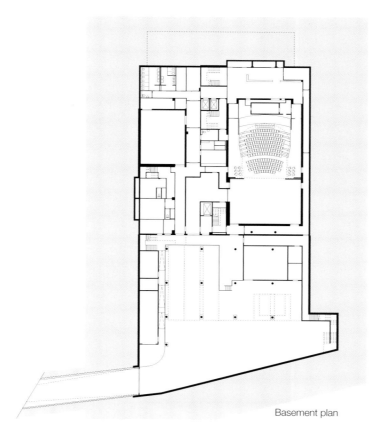

Basement plan

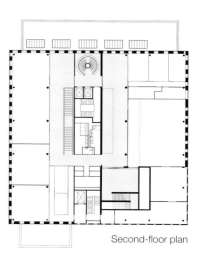

Second-floor plan

Opposite North–south section.

PROJECT DATA

LOCATION
Corby, Northamptonshire, UK

CLIENT
Corby Borough Council

SIZE
8,000 square metres

START DATE
2004

COMPLETION DATE
2010

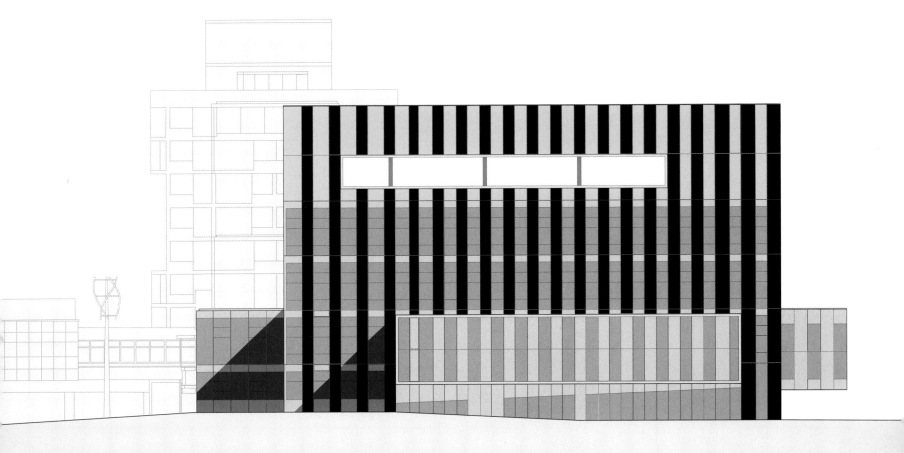

Opposite West elevation.

Above An early iteration of the
facade incorporated a light
installation by the artist Nayan
Kulkarni, intended to reflect the
continuation of the Cube below
ground. Funding complexities
meant that this element did
not go ahead.

Right The four active elevations of the Cube reflect its surroundings throughout the day and transform at night to reveal the interior.

Opposite The glazed facade is crucial to the environmental performance of the building. It is modulated according to orientation to limit solar heat gain and allow in light.

The council chamber and theatre circulation are clad in American black walnut boarding. The chamber features bespoke joinery and lighting, and a specially commissioned carpet by Timorous Beasties.

From below street level to the roof garden, an accessible promenade leads visitors through the building via a gentle ramp, 'lazy stair' and helical staircase.

Seth Rutt

At Hawkins\Brown, we believe that architecture isn't architecture until it's built. Of course we should celebrate and learn from the unbuilt idea – where concept hasn't been subjected to compromise – and many of our heroes have one foot planted firmly in the fecund world of academe, where paper architecture can take root and outlive built work. But if architecture is the harnessing of space, light and materials, then, for us, until a building becomes a tangible piece, it's just paper, pixels and promises.

It's not fashionable these days for an architect to have an ego. Hawkins\Brown has always eschewed the cliché of the incontrovertible genius architect in favour of an approach that is focused more on the client, the user and the context. But as a creative act, making a building that's any good requires continuity of authorship and a sense of ownership over the design. A collective ego – a sense of self-worth and belief in our work – gives us the tenacity to see projects through from conceptual studies to detailed construction drawings and advice on site.

Continuity of design control helps to retain a clear narrative, to create buildings and spaces that are legible with a clearly understood character. In tension with this is the tendency in the United Kingdom to switch architects during the process; it happens for many reasons, including changes in site ownership, lower fees and different skills between practices. But for us, remaining on a project throughout its construction enables us to incorporate buildability into future work as the feedback loop is maintained – so it's as much a desire for professional competency as the need to be credited as the design leader.

Ego aside, seeing a project through from beginning to end requires us to steer it through a process that involves many authors and contributors. Our efforts as a design leader rely heavily on the client and consultant team, and require the expertise of the site construction team to make an idea flesh – not to mention the client's and lender's money. So, to use other creative processes as a metaphor, perhaps we are screenwriters, directors and editors of a large-scale film production, rather than the sole author of a book.

Of the myriad individuals who contribute to and collaborate on a project, it's the client who is with us every step of the way, playing the role of the producer (to continue the film-making analogy). And if the client is a co-author, then their needs are an equal part of the creative process. But a good client will have a sense of social responsibility, and recognize that they are making a building for other people, one that should have a positive impact on its environment. For us, a successful project involves symbiosis between client and architect, and that should in turn spread across the wider team.

So far so idealistic, but the job of making a building is a tough, sometimes grubby affair. Human nature decrees that all involved in the process of creating a building – and let's not forget third parties, who may have valid reasons to resist – will want something different. The closer the alignment of desires among its participants, the more successful a project.

Our appointment is often on a tranched basis, so that discontinuity of authorship is always a threat to our involvement. The planning consent stage marks a fulcrum in the creative process, when a building concept is supposedly fixed, but the detail is yet to emerge. This is the point when developer clients may choose to pocket the change in value of a site, rather than take the risk of developing it. Similarly, the construction tender stage is a tipping point that divides many architects into 'concept' and 'delivery' practices.

In most architectural projects in the United Kingdom, the risk and detail design is transferred to the construction team, so it's understandable that they will want to work with an architect that gives them the information they need to build a project on time and safeguard their profit. Very large sums of money are at risk, so wider concerns beyond the construction phase – such as continuity of concept, beauty, joy, legibility and the personality of the building – fall down the ladder of priorities.

In architecture, we see a difference across the sectors. Typically, university buildings are developed with an estates and user group team that will inhabit a bespoke building designed for them, and there is a much greater chance that we will continue to be involved. However, in the commercial world – especially in speculative housing – we often see a switch in teams at gateways in the process, especially the planning stage. There is also a misapprehension among some clients that the planning stage represents completion of concept, and that the detail design stage does not fundamentally endanger the design.

Volume housebuilders are more fractured than most organizations. Many are divided into four groups that pass a project on from one stage to the next, from the land-buying team,

Why We Need to Build

to planning, then to construction, with the sales team arriving in the middle and towards the end. The first three – purchasing, planning and construction – tend to work with their favoured architects. Since the separate teams are individual profit centres, they tend to appoint practices that they've worked with before.

With many contractors and volume housebuilders, there is a sense of mistrust of 'concept' architects, a perception that such practices lack the detailing skill or alignment with the construction team's mission to get the project built on time and not lose money. This often brings the 'concept' architect – the guardian of the client's needs – into conflict with the construction team. Perhaps this is how good architecture gets built; apocryphal stories of our respected peers portray them more as street fighters using every dirty trick in the book to get the best result.

But it needn't be this way. At Hawkins\Brown, we don't subscribe to the idea of 'concept' and 'delivery' architects. We embrace the difficulty of transferring our responsibility to the contractor, and we respect the fact that they are managing risk for large sums of money and paying our bills. The best design-and-build projects connect us with the subcontractors so that we get the benefit of their experience and a better understanding of where the cost and construction challenges lie. It's easier to accept compromise if you're part of the team discussing it and helping to steer the process to safeguard quality. Often, especially for projects in the education sectors, we divide into two teams: a primary site-delivery team working for the contractor, and a monitoring team representing the original client. It takes

a professional attitude to avoid a perceived conflict of interest.

If we are not novated to the contractor, we are often retained as 'design guardian', to monitor compliance with our tender drawings and, more importantly, to advise and to help solve problems as they arise. This is a compromise that we are prepared to make, since we will make much of even limited involvement to steer a project and keep it true to the original design intent.

While I was writing this, a leading developer said that architects were in danger of 'being wiped out', owing to disengagement with the construction process. Certainly, as far as site delivery goes, it appears there will be a growing tendency towards a division between concept and delivery practices. We still think we can do both, however. We're increasingly designing our buildings to accommodate off-site manufacture and volumetric construction, and our use of Building Information Modelling in the early stages of design gives us a more direct connection to the built product.

It's amazing to see the difference in attitude and energy from our staff in the early design stages of a project if they know they're going to be there to see it built. Every detail matters more if we're going to be held to account towards the end of a project: technical strategy is explored more deeply than is absolutely necessary, and the avoidable but ubiquitous 'value-engineering' (read cost-cutting) process becomes something to engage in, so that we are among the authors of the compromise.

Conversely, the news that we won't be engaged after the planning or tender stages leads to heartbreak and a sense of

wasted time, since at this stage we will have been creatively involved for at least two years. It's common for creative people to anthropomorphize their work, since it contains their energy – a part of their soul. An extreme analogy of losing creative contact with a project, then, is a parent parting with a child. We always want to be there to raise a project and mould it into its final form.

If making a building is compared to giving birth and seeing a child grow, we'll mould it at the beginning and give it the essential programming and love. But we also want to be there to raise the unruly teenager into a recognizable member of our creative family.

Here East has transformed the former Press and Broadcast centres in the Queen Elizabeth Olympic Park into just over 103,000 square metres of space for London's creative and digital industries. Building on the spirit of neighbouring Hackney Wick, tech giants and universities sit alongside start-ups, artists and designers. They work and play in a network of spaces that have been designed with creative collisions in mind, supported by locally owned cafes, restaurants and bars.

A creative campus

In August 2012, as they came to a close, the Summer Olympics were wholeheartedly declared a success. The next step was to build a legacy. That was a simple enough undertaking when it came to those buildings that had been designed with a purpose and future ambition in mind, but it was less easy to decide what to do with the buildings that had housed thousands of broadcasters, photographers and journalists during the event.

The Media Centre site had been designed with economy and a specific purpose in mind, and the gargantuan windowless, steel-framed Broadcast Centre posed a real problem. At 275 metres long it would easily fit four jumbo jets, but that statistic did not add up to much when it came to planning for the future of the site. A competition call went out from iCity, a joint venture between the property investor Delancey and the data-centre operator Infinity SDC, to find an architect to match their ambition to transform the Media Centre site into a place for London's creative minds and digital agencies.

Hawkins\Brown are no strangers to designing for engagement, interaction and collaboration, and in fact that drives much of their work. The only question was whether they could do it at this scale.

Designing an ecosystem

Hackney Wick has been the home of innovation for centuries. Within its patchwork of industrial buildings, artists, designers and start-ups have bedded down and their entrepreneurial spirit, combined with unprecedented artistic output, has cemented the district's reputation. Hawkins\Brown took inspiration from this tightly knit community and transferred it to the huge buildings on the Media Centre site, breaking the structures down to make them more manageable, social and dynamic – ultimately, to make them more human. Here East is a natural extension of Hackney Wick, with an ecosystem that incubates a staggering range of businesses, buoyed by the Canalside, a 'life-support system' of bars, cafes and restaurants.

In order to design a campus where people could come together and do great things, the architects met artists and various business representatives. Such meetings gave them an understanding of the particular sorts of space those people need to do their work and to excel.

The ground floor of the Press Centre has been transformed into an Innovation Hub offering more than 6,000 square metres of co-working space, fitted out by Grimshaw. The Media Conference Room, known as 'The Theatre', is a 950-seat auditorium for product launches, talks, screenings, exhibitions and presentations, while the Broadcast Centre, providing nearly 80,000 square metres of space, is home to BT Sport, Ford and Loughborough University's London campus. University College London (UCL) has also taken up residence in the Broadcast Centre, where it carries out its groundbreaking research into advanced fabrication, robotics and engineering. The space, designed by Hawkins\Brown, is one of many projects the architects have worked on with UCL (see pages 11–23).

Of all the spaces on the campus, perhaps the Gantry exemplifies the joint spirit of Hackney Wick and Here East. Housed on the east elevation of the Broadcast Centre, it once supported several tonnes of air-handling equipment, but it has been reimagined as a 'cabinet of curiosities', providing affordable shed-like structures for a variety of designers, craftspeople and artists. The spaces have been designed as a collaboration between Hawkins\Brown and the local practice Architecture 00, using WikiHouse code, an open-source timber building system that can be customized to suit the unique needs of each user.

Opposite Here East is a monumental billboard for innovation, and its vast scale becomes clear when it is seen from above in the context of the Queen Elizabeth Park.

Right The sky sign announces Here East to those arriving at the park from Stratford station.

Here East

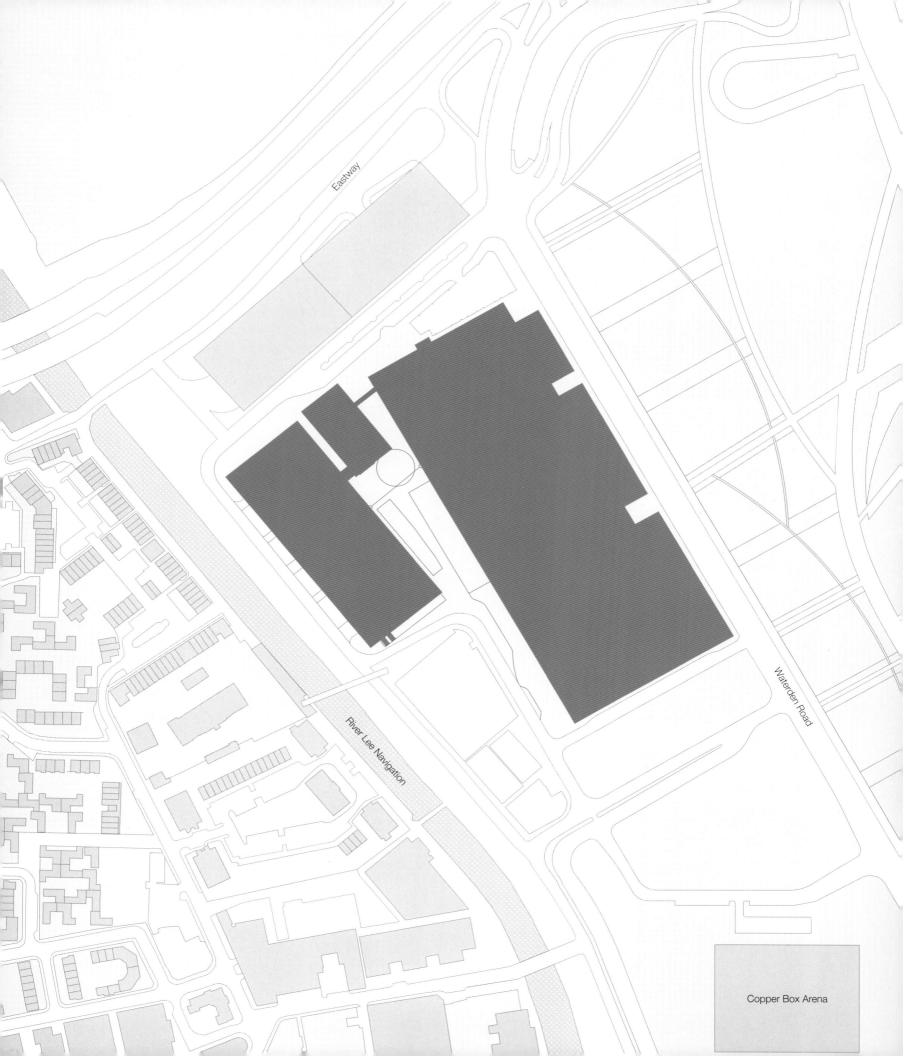

Eastway

River Lee Navigation

Waterden Road

Copper Box Arena

Central to the success of the design is the breaking down of the monolithic structure of the Broadcast Centre, which is achieved by the design's 'crust and core' concept. The original windowless facade has been stripped off and replaced with a double-glazed curtain-walling system, visually and physically opening it up to form routes through and create views between buildings. A 16-metre-deep perimeter 'crust' maximizes daylight, ventilation and views. This 'crust' surrounds a core that houses a massive data centre, state-of-the-art broadcast studios and UCL's centre for cross-disciplinary research.

More than 3,000 unique panels of curtain walling weighing in at about 450 tonnes cover the new south, west and east elevations. The panels, wrapped in a complex frit pattern made up of more than eight million ceramic dots, were designed in collaboration with Poke, one of the world's most highly respected digital design agencies. The pattern was inspired by the dazzle camouflage painted on ships during the First World War to confuse enemy submarines, producing a disruptive and bold graphic treatment that breaks the facade down into more human-sized sections while staying in harmony with the ethos of the campus. Holes punched into the building break up the frontage and create openings and atriums, and the floor-to-ceiling heights are humanized with mezzanines that create a variety of spaces.

When the Media Centre site was first developed, there was little 'legacy' in mind. During the Games, what is now the buzzing Canalside was carpeted in barbed wire to prevent ticketless punters from trying to sneak in. Now there's no barbed wire or boundary fence. Instead, Here East has made its own legacy for the city: a home where the brightest and boldest come together to make great things.

Opposite Site plan, showing the Press Centre (left), the Theatre (centre) and the Broadcast Centre and the Gantry (right).

This page Before and after photographs of the Press and Broadcast centres. The Broadcast Centre has undergone the most dramatic transformation, and now accommodates a rich mix of activities.

Right The Gantry is an example of collaborative data-driven design. The cladding for each studio unit references the site's industrial heritage.

Below West elevation of the Broadcast Centre.

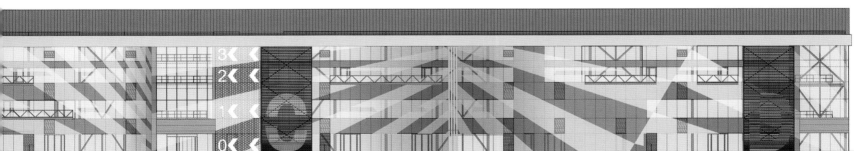

Right Ground-floor plan.

Below A long section through the Gantry and the Broadcast and Press centres demonstrates the scale and variety of the spaces.

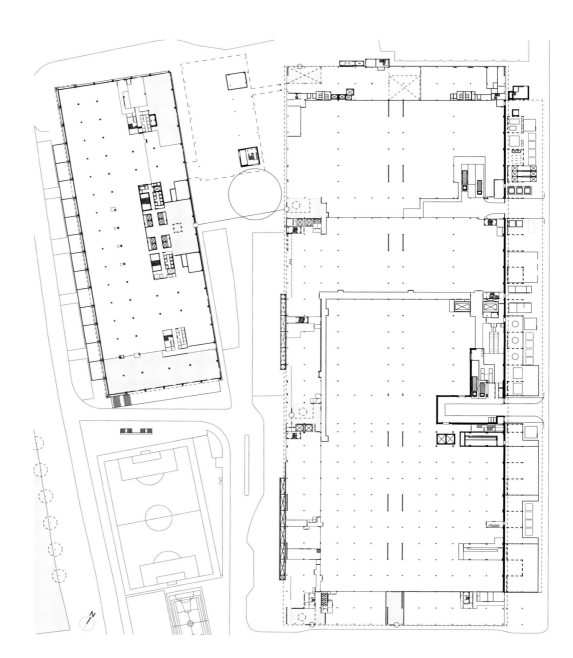

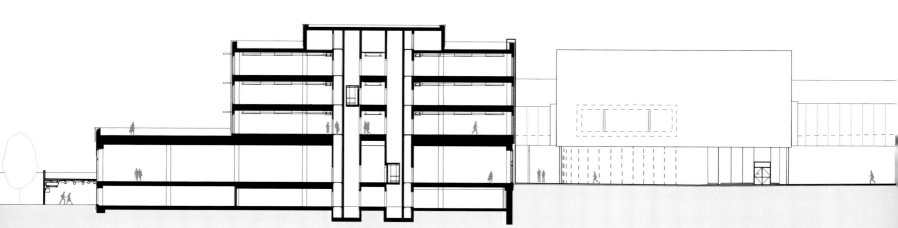

PROJECT DATA

LOCATION
Queen Elizabeth Olympic Park,
Stratford, London

CLIENT
Innovation City (London) Ltd;
Delancey

SIZE
103,000 square metres

START DATE
2013

COMPLETION DATE
2018

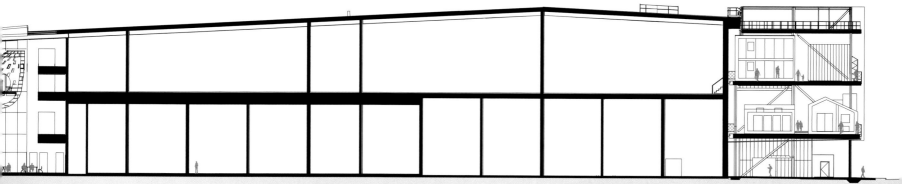

Twenty-metre-high panels mark the Broadcast Centre entrances, referencing aircraft hangars and industrial warehouses.

Right The cafe, bar and shops of the Press Centre face soft canal-side landscaping, and are home to a thriving community of local, independent businesses.

Below The bright colours, playful graphics and raw public realm at Here East reference the creative energy of Hackney Wick, overlapped with the scale and openness of the park.

Above The scale of the Broadcast Centre provided the opportunity to create large floor-to-ceiling heights and light-filled atria with walkways and suspended meeting pods.

Right Each of the three main receptions in the Broadcast Centre references industrial materials and fabrication, including steel, timber and fabric.

Above The main reception area of the Press Centre is flexible and is used for informal working, meetings, talks, events and product launches.

Left The generous heights of the Press Centre interior allowed substantial mezzanines in the Plexal Innovation Centre and the Here East management and marketing suite.

Hilden Grange Preparatory School in Tonbridge had outgrown its tired facilities, and pupils were housed in dilapidated temporary classrooms. The school desperately needed good learning environments that matched its ambition. Hawkins\Brown's design for the new Ritblat Building embraces the steep slope of the site, which overlooks the Kent Weald, to create a well-crafted new school that celebrates its surroundings.

All too often, pupils are shoehorned into buildings that have outgrown their use, or are siloed away in temporary classrooms, leaving them disconnected and unable to realize their full potential. This was true of Hilden Grange; its pupils were cut off not only from one another but also from the nature that surrounded them.

Any design would have to create connections to the existing Victorian school buildings and overcome the site's steep slope, as well as allay locals' concerns that they would end up with a building out of tune with the town's green and leafy surroundings. They needn't have worried. The architects have played to the strengths of the site, disguising the mass of the building by inserting it into the landscape and giving it wings that stretch out towards the Weald beyond.

Creating potential

A sizeable chunk of the budget was spent on the necessary groundworks, so the design had to work hard to squeeze every last drop out of the remaining funds. The newly named Ritblat Building comprises two low wings that extend perpendicularly from the existing school into the landscape across three diminishing levels. Connections between the levels are made by external walkways or landscaped 'terraces'. New accommodation includes specialist art and science classrooms, a library and a new assembly/dining hall sunk into the slope between the two wings. The hall, which is big enough for the whole school to assemble in, has wide glass doors that open on to external dining areas and an outdoor amphitheatre.

It is clear that care and attention have gone into every element of the design, from the crafting and construction of the wings to the choice of planting. Internally, the building is simple and honest; the timber structure is left visible, with plenty of space that pupils and teachers can make their own.

Fast track

Construction on an operational site is never easy, even less when children are involved. In order to increase speed and efficiency, most of the new school building was constructed from prefabricated cross-laminated timber (CLT). Although it was used extensively across Europe in the 1990s and 2000s, CLT was a relatively new construction material in the United Kingdom at the time, especially when used as an exposed finish. Most of the components were manufactured off-site and assembled as a kit of parts, all within a single academic year, so the build caused minimal disruption to day-to-day learning or to the school's neighbours. Not only was this a fast method, but also it created well-insulated, naturally ventilated classrooms and learning spaces using a sustainable material. Plus, the pupils saw the CLT pieced together in front of their eyes, like a giant jigsaw.

Guided by nature

Carefully considered landscaping and materials ground the building while weaving it neatly into its context. Working with B|D Landscape Architects, Hawkins\Brown have created a school that is as much about the outside as it is about the inside. The external walkways encourage movement, so that students pass one another while moving between classrooms, going to lunch or playing.

Each wing is made distinctive through its materials. The west wing, with a pitched roof that echoes the Victorian school building, is covered in traditional cedar shingles and rainscreen cladding. This produces a

Opposite The exposed internal timber structure helps children to understand how the building has been constructed as a well-insulated, sustainable learning environment.

Below The extensive green roof of the east wing includes species from the surrounding Weald.

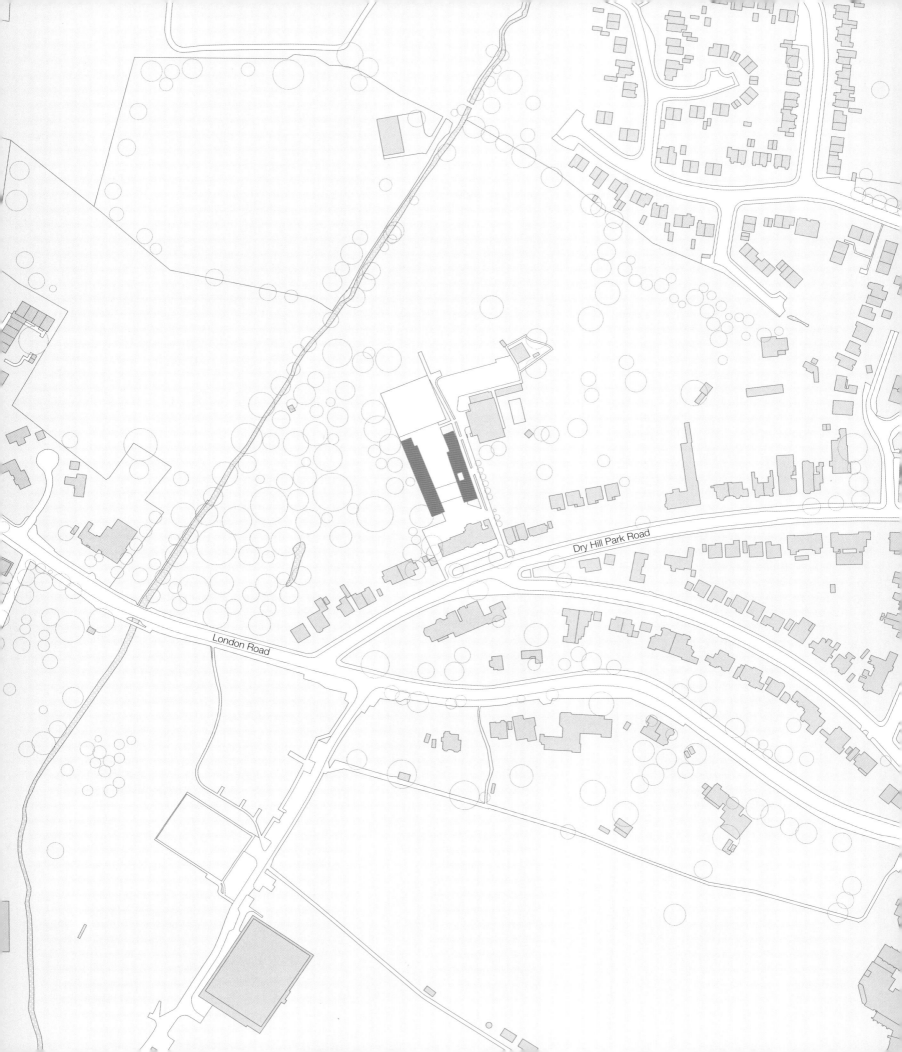

Dry Hill Park Road

London Road

quality of seamlessness that grounds the school in its surroundings. The east wing, clad with vertical strips of larch, is topped with an undulating green meadow roof that helps it to blend into the landscape while also softening the building's mass.

What makes the Ritblat Building so special is its celebration of nature and play. Everywhere are gestures that open up the building: the framing of views, external circulation, visual connections across the building and bold planting. The possibility of play is everywhere, since learning and play spaces are not demarcated but instead intertwine and extend through and across the building. Terraces spill out from classrooms, and the colourful landscape undulates and morphs between the wings, planted with Scots pine and birch trees that provide shelter and shade while echoing the woods beyond.

Green outside and in

The building achieved a BREEAM Very Good rating, and the approach was driven by the client's desire to spend money and attention on the areas that would make a real difference to the daily experience of pupils and staff. The key areas of focus were materials, ventilation and landscaping. The building is entirely naturally ventilated, and the windows are arranged to offer high- and low-level ventilation across the far east and west facades. Geotextile-reinforced wild-flower banks and the biodiverse green roof add to the ecological credentials and respond to local biodiversity action plans.

The new school was completed in 2012 and has rooted itself firmly into the landscape. Its pupils, aged from three to thirteen, are enjoying their stimulating and secure new environment; they are reportedly calmer, more focused and more eager to learn than ever before. No longer disconnected, they now have a school that has been designed to help them realize their academic and creative potential through learning, play and access to nature.

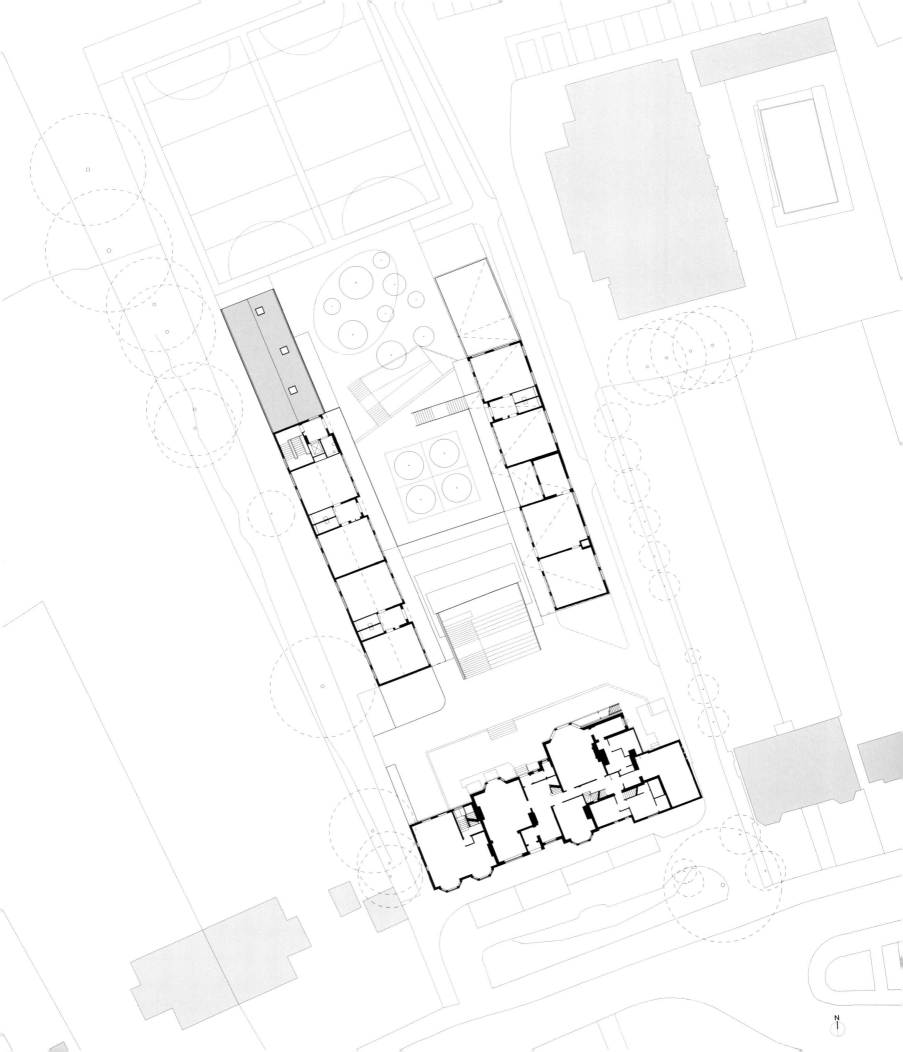

Opposite Ground-floor plan.

Below South–north section
through the west wing.

PROJECT DATA

LOCATION
Tonbridge, Kent, UK

CLIENT
Alpha Plus Group; Hilden Grange
Preparatory School

SIZE
1,473 square metres

START DATE
2010

COMPLETION DATE
2012

Children enjoy playing, learning and socializing in their new environment.

Top The picture windows of the east wing highlighted at dusk.

Above The striking timber cladding of both wings is seen with the Victorian school building in the background.

Overleaf The Ritblat Building from above, with far-reaching views to the north.

Darryl Chen

Space to think

Working in an architectural practice is dictated by an increasingly complex set of routines. Undoubtedly the tyranny of the project programme leads us at both an individual and a corporate level to optimize our actions. How else do we produce what we have been asked for? And so we lean on habits that make us efficient, and bat back the barrage of emails and alerts that constantly nibble away at our working day. This melange of sketching, drafting, mocking up, marking up, typing, discussing, instructing and imploring is the sum total of the architect's day.

Research, most architects agree, occurs somewhere in among these dutiful processes. However, in our studio we've come to realize that there are greater returns to be had from treating research as a distinct activity. This kind of research is self-directed, open-ended. It requires a space outside project programmes to gestate and develop. At Hawkins\Brown we've come to characterize our research activity as nothing more or less than a space to think.

Don't get me wrong: of course we think through doing. But this doing is distinct from normal architectural activity. It draws on a set of skills that are familiar to the architect and yet outside the normal core activities: long-form reading, knowing the difference between correlation and causation, the methodical collation of information, arguing, thinking critically (or situating a set of knowledge within related discourses), finding and not fudging evidence, and asking the right questions.

Jumps and sidesteps

Research defined on those terms allows us to advance our thinking to a much broader horizon of objectives. By taking on larger questions, we create new knowledge that takes us to sometimes surprising places.

Research is a constant tension between intuition and rigour. A project might start with a piece of gossip, an overheard conversation, a hunch about why something is the way it is. If it persists in the mind for long enough (how many 'great' ideas in the pub never make it out of the door?), intrigues enough colleagues and continues to be under-represented in the industry at large, it is probably a hunch worth pursuing. The rest is testing the hypothesis, turning it upside down until something falls out.

Our hunches generally lead to the big questions – broad shifts in architectural typology that are aligned to changes in our society or economy. I believe the answers to those questions have the greatest implications for the architectural profession.

We map trends that are wide enough to apply across whole sectors, and we also apply practical outcomes for the design of individual projects. The results of our research are somewhere between immediately applicable insights for architectural design, and longer meditations that frame our projects over years.

Not bound by the scrutiny of public-service agreements to demonstrate 'value outcomes', we are content (for now) to let our research relate to our wider design practice in a relatively unstructured manner. The steady stream of insight, evidence, contention, speculation, provocation and dead ends that characterizes our research fuels the jumps and sidesteps of our practice's design evolution.

In our report 'Emperor's New Housing' (2013), we disputed the idea that London's future housing should be driven by aesthetics. Working deliberately outside the constraints of the London Housing Design Guide and critiquing the developing 'new London vernacular', we put forward four housing prototypes, each of which responds to an emerging London demographic. As we continue to work on a broad range of residential projects across the capital, we are seeing those four housing types being realized as viable development products, and we are continuing to have conversations with developers about new models of living for the near future. We anticipated a shift in the conversation from aesthetics and regulation to disruptive solutions that meet the needs of new household types.

In 2015 we set out to understand creative workplaces from a variety of critical and design-led perspectives. In 'Creative Ecologies', we mapped the history of the office with an emphasis on co-working as the currently dominant paradigm. We positioned our own Here East (see pages 39–49) as an example of how the accepted model of co-working space is becoming richer and more closely integrated into its urban environment. At the scale of the office, we collaborated with technologists to enable live data gathering, in order to understand how workers use space. We become guinea pigs ourselves, subjecting our own staff to being tracked from desk to meeting room to corridor chat.

In 2017 we undertook a commission from the British Council for Offices to research the latest trends in office receptions. 'First Impressions' was a compilation of literature survey, quantitative data, interviews,

The Practice of Thinking

case studies and design speculation that identified the reception as a site of increasing convergence with hotel lobbies, co-working hubs and public squares. Charting a trajectory of change allowed us to make a proposition about how whole office buildings might evolve in the future.

&\also …

Witness the rise of the #thoughtleader, a term that is now tainted with the corporate blandness of so many smiling headshots on a conference handout. Intended to be attached to someone who leads because of the quality of their knowledge in a particular field, it has become a byword for that special place where corporate marketing machine meets senior manager ego. #thoughtleadership is like the second prize for anyone who dreamed of being a capital-C Consultant, someone who could boast that their sole job was to spout wisdom, and send eye-watering bills to clients for the privilege.

Hawkins\Brown's think tank, &\also, is driven by a spirit of enquiry. Our output helps to frame the circumstances in which we build, and to make design better. Operating like a practice within a practice and fuelled by dedicated core personnel, we assist our architects in doing some of the thinking that is crowded out of their busy days.

We tap into the urge of every architect to make her intervention in this world count towards a better and more coherent place. We want to join others who share that ideal. And we use our research as a space to think, to unpack not only how we do that, but also why. We have an expanded notion of what architecture can be and how it can be achieved. Will the brief get you where you want to go? What else should this building do? Is a building even the answer? By thinking between briefs and setting our own agenda, the think tank helps the studio to go beyond a regular architect's remit.

The think tank was named after a guiding idea that formed the title of our practice's first monograph, published in 2003. It sums up the plurality, interdisciplinarity and additionality that are championed in the research think tank: &\also.

The Bob Champion Research and Education Building sets the tone for new development in Norwich Research Park, a site full of prestigious institutes carrying out pioneering scientific research. Completed in just twelve months with a modest budget, it is testament to what can be achieved when client, architect, project manager and contractor are united in a shared ambition. The building is a collaboration between the University of East Anglia, one of the world's leading research-led universities, the Norfolk and Norwich University Hospitals NHS Foundation Trust, R.G. Carter Limited and the Bob Champion Cancer Trust. The new laboratories house 'translational' or 'bench to bedside' research that uses medical discoveries made in the lab to create treatments that can fight diseases in the hospital.

A new home

The university's medical school was in urgent need of a new home. Students were cycling or taking the bus to the hospital from the main campus, 20 kilometres away. Between ward visits they had to sit on the floor in the corridors, taking up valuable medical space, since there was nowhere else for them to go. In the face of these operational problems, it was imperative for the university and the hospital to get funding in place as quickly as possible for a new building.

With such a tight budget and programme, the team had to understand the client's vision and ambition fully from the start if they were to develop a concept that could secure funding in parallel with producing construction drawings. Hawkins\Brown therefore undertook a comprehensive briefing process, during which they met stakeholders including hospital staff, lecturers, postgraduate researchers and students, as well as patients and visitors.

Designing for innovation

There is no doubt that this building works hard for the money. Carefully considered spaces make the most of the budget, and cash was spent in the areas where the users would reap most benefit. Access is via an atrium entered from the sunny south-facing courtyard, or through the car park to the rear – handy for those visiting patients. This new landscaped public space is part of a walking route that climbs down the bank from a pedestrian crossing on the busy road, making it easy for people to come and go between the hospital and the new building.

The atrium, with its public cafe on the ground floor, its sweeping staircase and its spectacular views, is the social heart of the building. In this engaging space, artwork influenced by microscopic bone structures rises to the lecture theatre, reminding visitors of the innovative medical research that is taking place around them. As one would expect of a Hawkins\Brown building, there are break-out and social spaces on every floor, providing fertile ground for people to meet, discuss ideas, listen and learn. The design maximizes opportunities for creative collisions and collaboration, from the curvy central staircase and cafe to the research areas and even the courtyard garden.

The atrium links the two wings into which the building is split both organizationally and physically. One wing, two storeys high, is dedicated to laboratory research, a lecture theatre and a 'biobank' for the storage of tissue samples from across the site. The other, teaching, wing is three naturally ventilated storeys of shared learning spaces, medical simulation wards and write-up areas. North-facing skylights in its sawtooth roof flood the open-plan second floor with natural light, while south-facing photovoltaic panels generate electricity for the building.

The design embraces a long-term, flexible, holistic approach to sustainability. It makes the best use of natural resources for heating, cooling and ventilation, creating a comfortable internal atmosphere while achieving the high performance standards the university sets for all its buildings.

Opposite The main entrance to the new building, which houses the research team of the Bob Champion Cancer Research Laboratory. The laboratory is supported by the Bob Champion Cancer Trust, which was set up in 1983 by an award-winning jockey who had recovered from testicular cancer.

Below The sculptural staircase in the entrance brings together everyone who uses the building in one welcoming space.

Bob Champion Research and Education Building

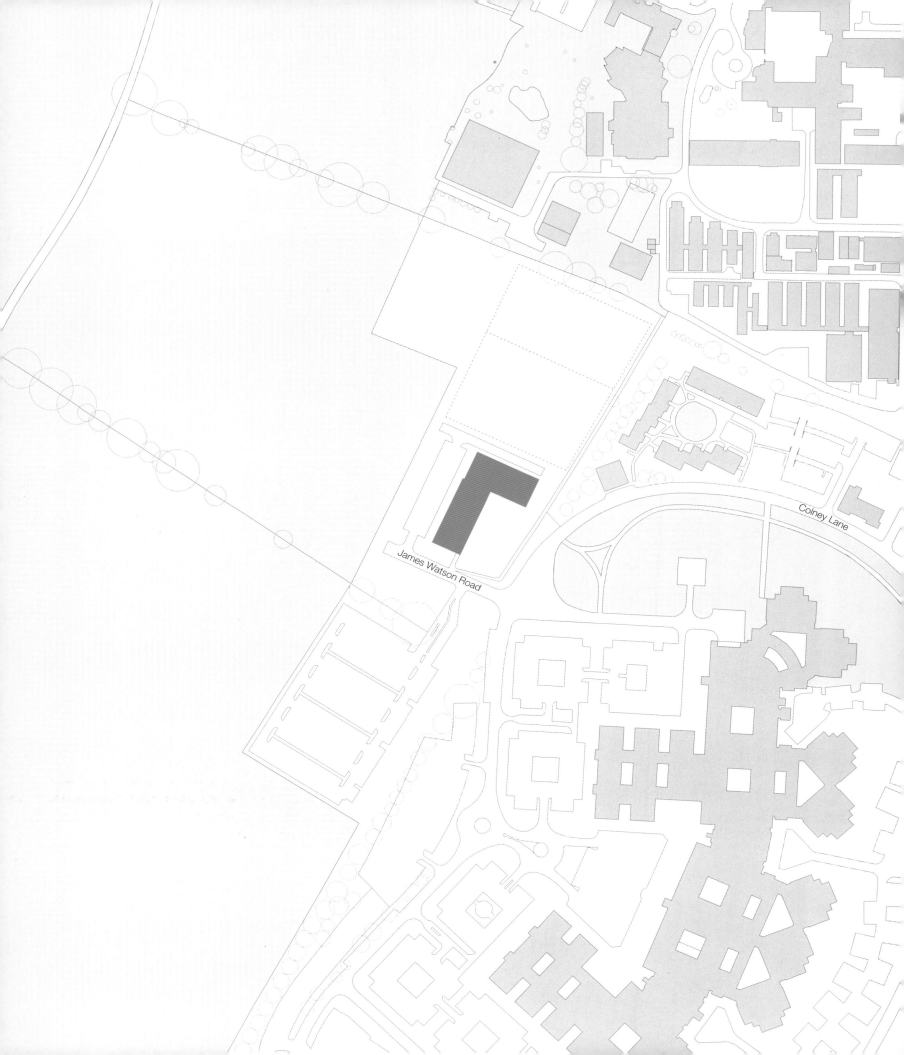

James Watson Road

Colney Lane

Right A section through the building shows the laboratory wing (right) separated from the teaching and social spaces, to meet the specialized environmental requirements of each function.

Below A construction image shows the roof forms clearly, before the timber skin was wrapped around the building.

Grounded in nature

This, Hawkins\Brown's largest building in a 'rural' setting, draws inspiration from farm buildings and industrial sheds. The speed of the design process and the references to the structure and materials of sheds, barns and outbuildings kept the building form direct and straightforward.

As gutsy as the design is, it plays to the strengths of its surroundings. The building responds to the long views across open fields, and appears to have bedded down in them, embracing the colours of the landscape and the way they change with the seasons, from yellow and ochre to rich brown earth and then verdant green. The architects' choice of materials was influenced by its closest neighbour, the John Innes research building. Nods to agri-industry typology are seen most clearly in the serrated roof and the slats of western red cedar that clad the wings. This prefabricated timber cladding, brought to the site and bolted on, kept construction on its fast schedule while ensuring its quality. The slats are attached on rails to unitized panels, and appear to float, bringing depth and interest to the elevation. Bands of windows are punched into the frame of the building and kept to a minimum, to mitigate heat gain from sunlight in the densely occupied spaces.

Inside, the materials and colours change subtly to demarcate the various parts of the building, creating an intuitive wayfinding system. Mustard, heather and corn-coloured upholstery complements the timber cladding and bespoke joinery of the atrium. These warm tones continue into the teaching wing, while the clinical facilities are marked by cooler shades of green and blue.

The Bob Champion Research and Education Building has won a clutch of local and national awards. For everyone involved, however, it is hard to imagine a greater accolade than knowing that the work going on inside is making a real difference to people's lives.

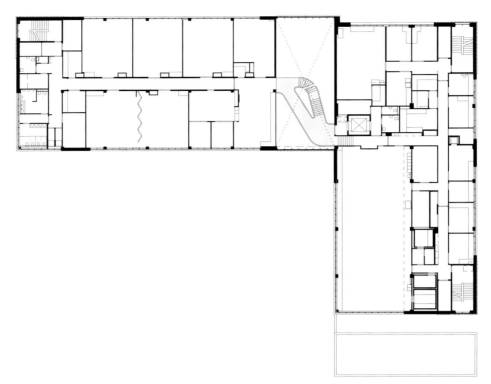

Upper-floor plan

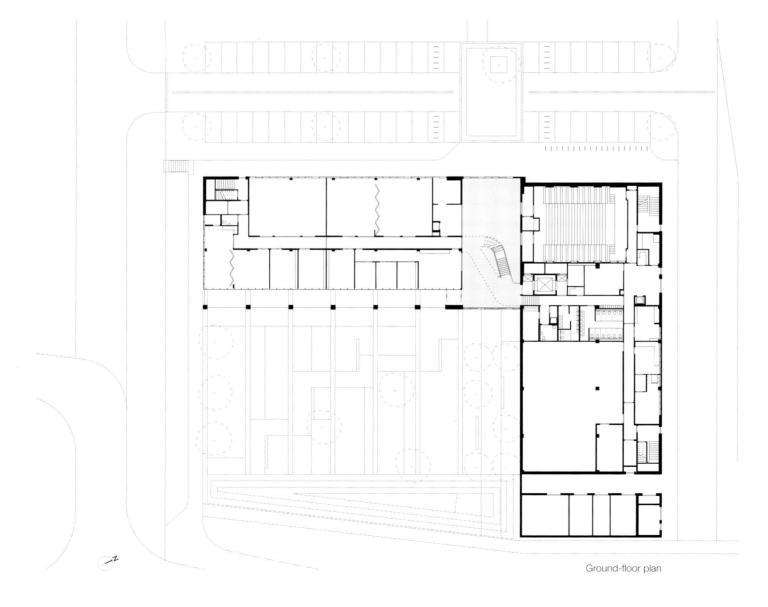

Ground-floor plan

A section shows the different
ceiling heights in the two wings.

PROJECT DATA

LOCATION
Norwich, Norfolk, UK

CLIENT
University of East Anglia Estates
and Buildings Division; Norfolk
and Norwich University Hospitals
NHS Foundation Trust; R.G. Carter
Limited; Bob Champion Cancer
Trust

SIZE
4,465 square metres

START DATE
2012

COMPLETION DATE
2014

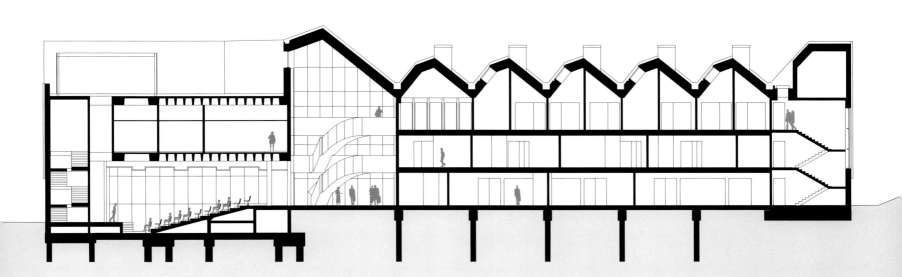

Right The rhythm of the western red cedar cladding battens varies across the facade, and includes a super-graphic 'UEA' that brands the building.

Below The materials and form anchor the building in its rural surroundings, and make it appear very different from other clinical research facilities.

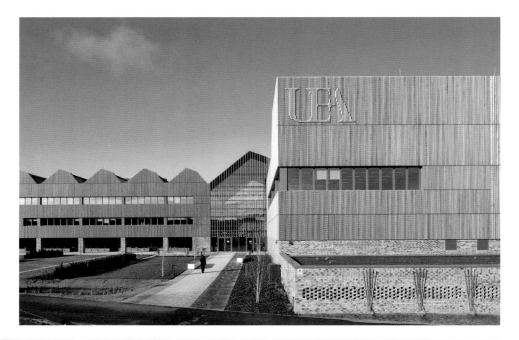

The timber cladding continues
across the glazed atrium to unite
the whole building in a single form,
while also providing solar shading.

The cafe set around the central staircase provides meeting and study space that creates a social centre for the building.

Above Open-plan study spaces look on to the atrium below, and out across the open fields that surround the building.

Left The naturally ventilated lecture theatre seats 200 people.

The new building with its landscaped southern courtyard, bordered by a sheltered arcade and pathway that link directly to the hospital.

Park Hill, the iconic Brutalist estate that looms over Sheffield, has been reinvigorated for the twenty-first century. Hawkins\Brown has brought back to life a building of great cultural and social importance, while staying true to the original spirit of the estate. More than that, the practice has created a place that is fit for Sheffield, a place of which the people can be proud.

Rebirth of an icon

Built between 1957 and 1961, the original 995-home estate exemplified the pioneering, bold new model of housing that was sweeping Europe. Park Hill was the vision of two young modernist architects, Jack Lynn and Ivor Smith, who believed that architecture had the power to solve society's problems. Famed for its 'streets in the sky' – the interconnected decks that aimed to bring traditional street life right to the doorsteps of elevated flats – Park Hill was beloved of its residents, who enjoyed the pubs and shops that made up the heart of the estate. But in the 1970s and 1980s the development began to suffer, and by the 1990s the once great building was demonized and ill-kept, the original community having broken apart and moved away.

For many, it seemed a foregone conclusion that Park Hill, in common with so many other post-war buildings, would be demolished. However, English Heritage had other ideas, and in 1998 the estate was listed, making it Europe's largest Grade II*-listed structure. Its future was assured.

The question now was what was next for this white elephant. It was Hawkins\Brown, together with the developer Urban Splash and collaborators Studio Egret West and Grant Associates, who took the bold steps that were necessary to transform Park Hill into a place where people would once more want to live. A plan was carefully conceived and developed to build on the character and potential of the building, while focusing on re-creating the community at the heart of the estate. It was essential to connect Park Hill once again to the surrounding landscape and to the city – no mean feat when many deemed it to be a blight on Sheffield's skyline.

A radical reinterpretation

Given the fact of its listing, the building's structure had to work hard, but fortunately the team had good bones to build on. The concrete frame, or 'grid' as it became known, was stripped back, cleaned and painstakingly patched with about 5,000 repairs.

The refurbishment has retained the integrity of the original structure, with four flats split over three floors, clustered around the concrete cores. The balconies' original concrete balustrades have been replaced with similar pre-cast versions topped with hardwood handrails, giving a lighter touch while maintaining the character of the building.

The most obvious change is the bold new facade. To win the city over, Park Hill had to reassert itself and once again make its mark on the world. Brightly coloured anodized aluminium panels and full-height glazing have replaced the original brickwork. The panels, in an array of iridescent colours, catch and reflect the light, transforming the estate into a beacon for the city.

Creating a community

Park Hill has created a sustainable mixed community of new homes for all kinds of family. The well-planned flats have been reinstated, subtly altered to create modern, open spaces. The architects retained and maximized the best qualities of the original design, which included natural ventilation, dual-aspect layout and south- and

Opposite Park Hill neighbours.

Below An archival photograph shows Ivor Smith's original development in the 1960s.

Park Hill

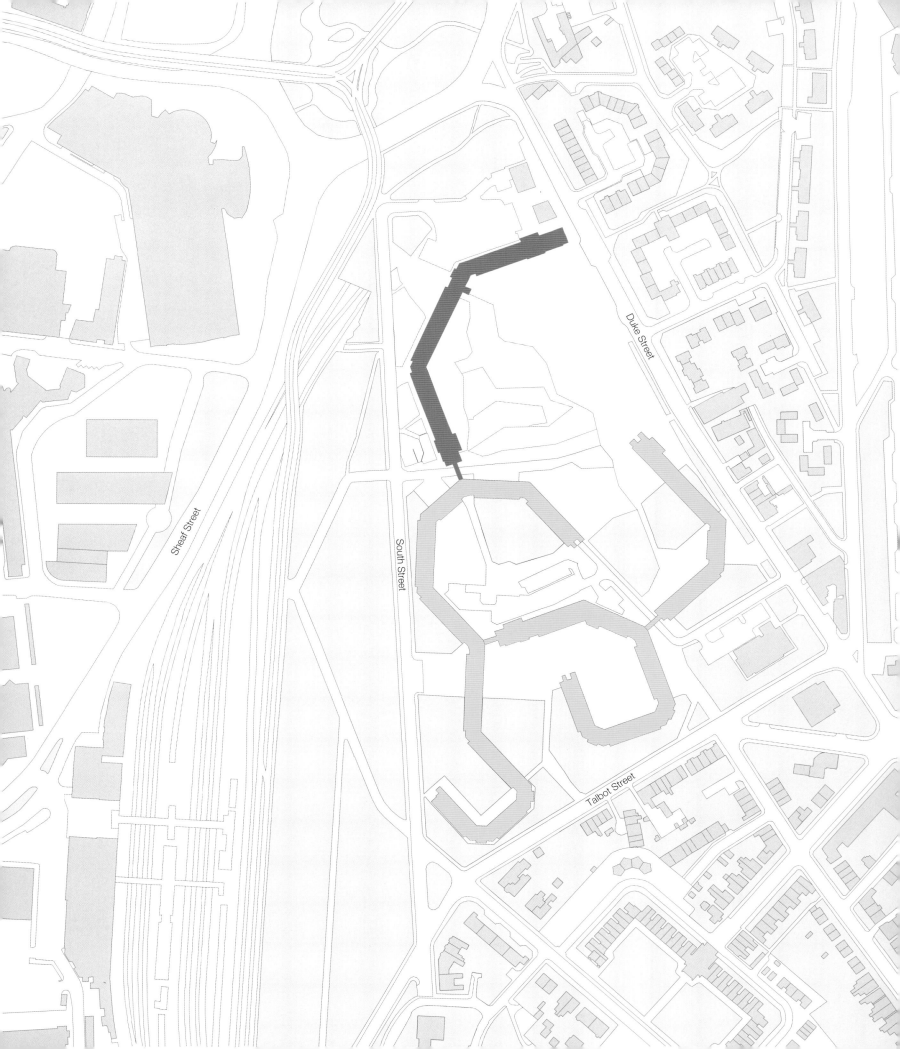

west-facing living areas filled with natural light. Every flat has its own generous private balcony, commanding wide views of the city. Internal spaces play on and celebrate the estate's Brutalist origins. Exposed structural walls and beams are juxtaposed with high-quality finishes and clever detailing.

The 'streets in the sky' are back, but now they are overlooked by windows from the flats, making them more sociable while providing passive surveillance. The 'streets' are served by two large glass panoramic lifts and a stainless-steel spiral staircase that wends its way through the frame of the building.

Park life

The lower three storeys are fully glazed on both sides, a clever move that opens up the building, allowing views out and through. These spaces are now home to thriving businesses that draw people to and through Park Hill and help to re-create the buzz of the estate's once thriving 'high street'. The Grace Owen Nursery School, the heart of Park Hill's community for more than fifty years, has also been relocated on the ground floor.

A striking 'cut' has been made through the building's concrete frame, creating a four-storey gap in the central lift core and forming a clear main entrance and gateway that welcomes people through the estate. A new paved walkway has also improved movement across the site, connecting with routes to the railway station and the city centre.

Park Hill always felt isolated from its surroundings, but it has now been grounded in its very own parkland and engages actively with the landscape. The green spaces, designed in collaboration with Grant Associates, include large trees and areas of loose natural planting that echo the rugged beauty of the nearby Peak District National Park.

The reinvigorated estate is a fitting tribute to the original architects' ambition to create a place that would benefit the people of Sheffield and improve their lives. It is once again a much-coveted place in the city, and one to be proud of.

Opposite The site plan shows the completed Phase 1 and the remaining footprint of the building.

Above A collage shows the original facade, the building stripped back to its core structure and the completed redevelopment.

Right The newly renovated Phase 1 of Park Hill, with Sheffield railway station in the foreground.

PROJECT DATA

LOCATION
Sheffield, Yorkshire, UK

CLIENT
Urban Splash; Sheffield City
Council; HCA; Great Places
Housing Group; English Heritage

SIZE
13,000 square metres

START DATE
2004

COMPLETION DATE
2015 (Phase 1)

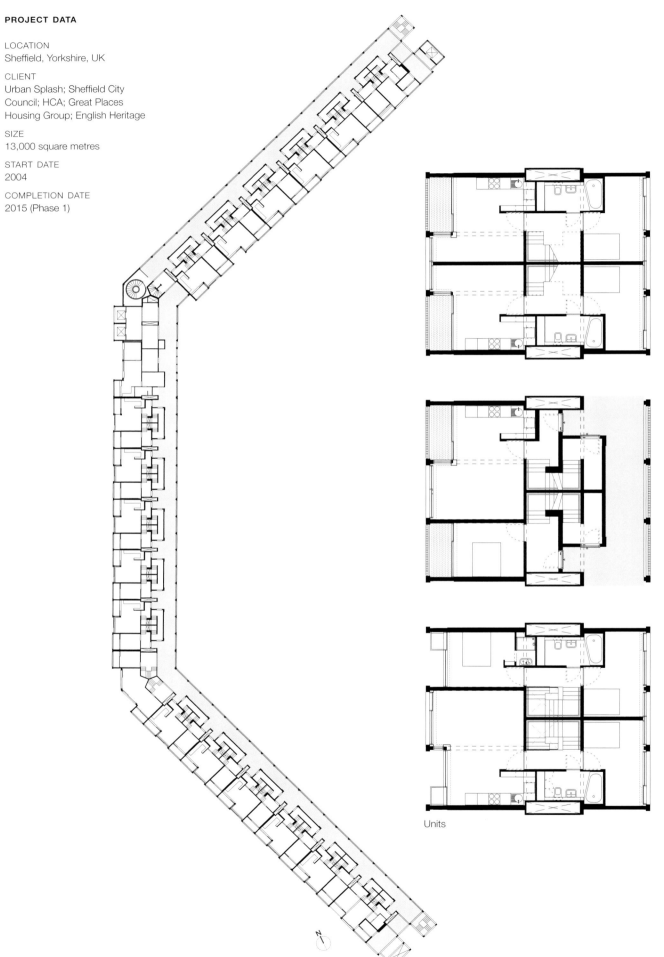

Units

Plan

Opposite A city-facing section
of Phase 1.

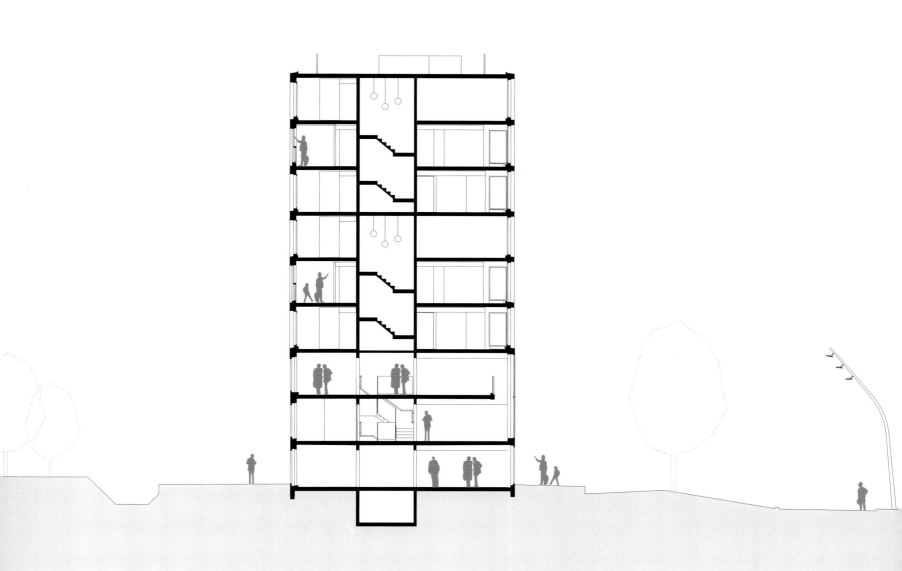

Left Coloured anodized aluminium panels sit within the armature of the original facade and are inspired by the brick tones of the 1950s scheme.

Below South elevation seen from Sheaf Square.

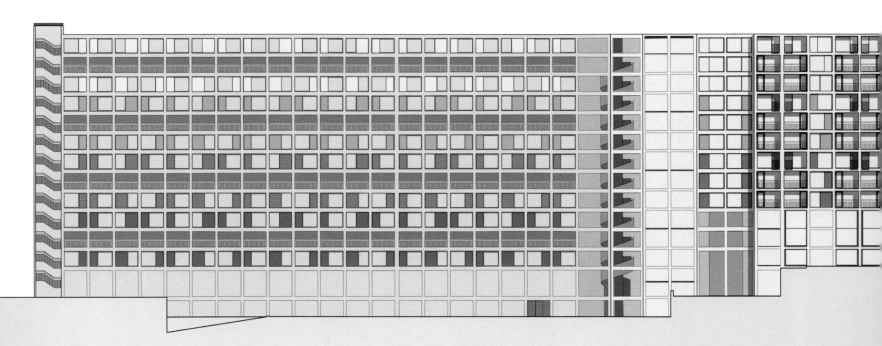

Overleaf Regenerated public realm and pedestrian routes lead to the main entrance.

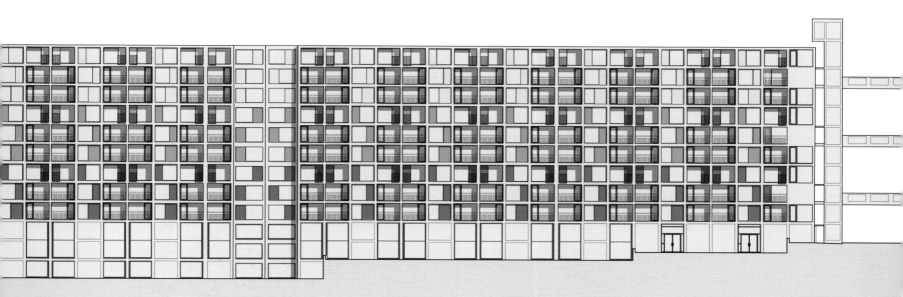

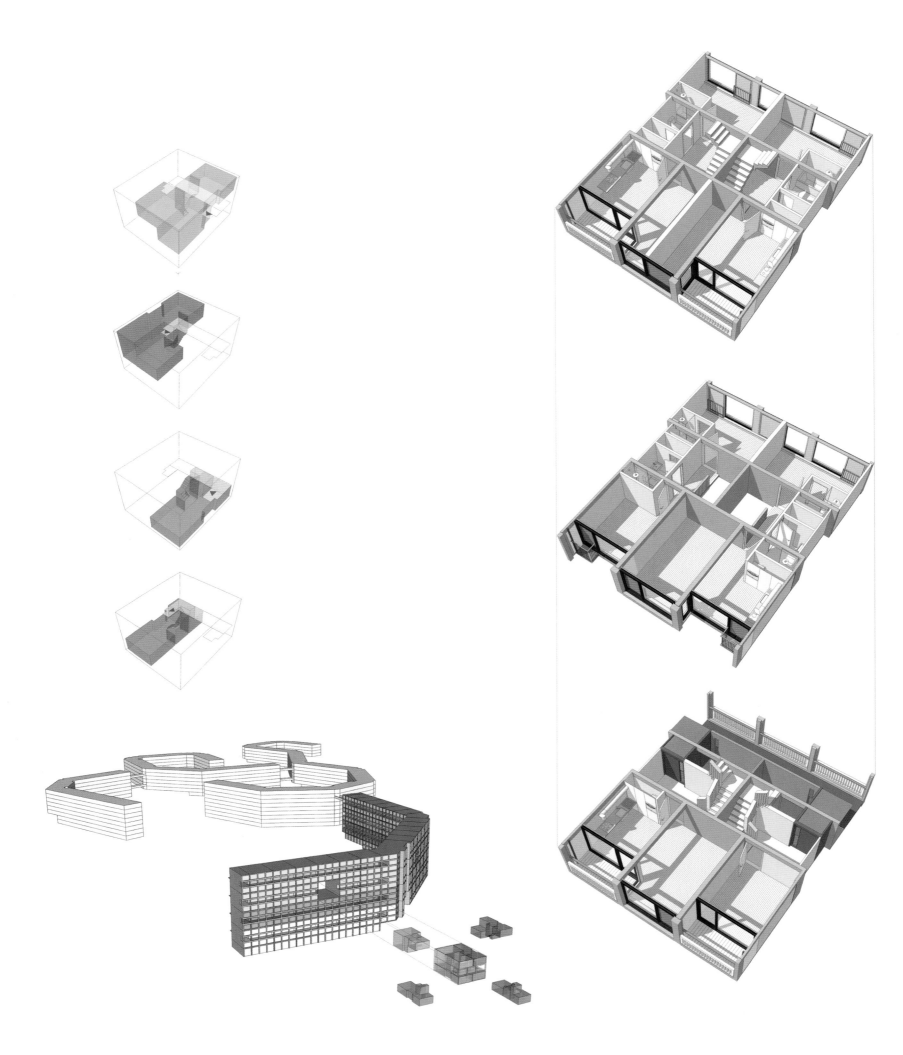

Left Exposed concrete walls in the refurbished flats reference the building's heritage, with contemporary flooring, fittings and fixtures.

Above Hawkins\Brown's interior design team fitted out a show flat with a celebration of designers who recycle, refashion and revalue old pieces of furniture.

Opposite An early diagram explains how the flats are arranged in clusters of four types.

Right The famed 'streets in the sky' form a 3.2-kilometre network enabling residents to walk under cover and on the flat around the whole neighbourhood.

Below A bold new four-storey entrance takes residents and visitors into the heart of Park Hill.

Below, right Residents began a competition to display their favourite, most outlandish objects in the windows on to the streets in the sky.

The new ground-level high street of art spaces, cafes, restaurants, offices and shops has revitalized the public realm for residents and visitors.

Nicola Rutt

To embark on any kind of refurbishment is to take a step into the unknown, and requires a very different mindset from that for a new-build. There is continuous dialogue between existing building and project team, sometimes calm and acquiescent, often argumentative and unpredictable. It is difficult to know how much the building will submit to the requirements of the brief, and how much it will resist. But from this struggle comes real creative opportunity.

A building's presence goes beyond the physical and plays a part in local history, ingrained to varying degrees in the memories of local people. Many buildings are in the background and go almost unnoticed until plans are made to alter or demolish them. Often, we do not realize that we care about a building, or have some level of emotional attachment to it, until it is threatened, when suddenly our memories come rushing to the front of our minds. The philosopher Alain de Botton describes how works of architecture 'talk to us' in his foreword to *Architectural Voices* by David Littlefield and Saskia Lewis (2007). His theory is that our attraction to a building is more than aesthetic, relating also to 'certain moods that they seek to encourage' and 'an attraction to a particular way of life' that the building promotes through its architectural features.

When we talk about the spirit of a place, we are referring to its meaning and symbolism. A town hall, for example, represents civic pride and continuity with the past. It is also a place where the experiences of the local community range from the joyous celebration of a wedding to the painful registration of a death. Working with buildings that evoke such strong personal feelings throughout the community must always be more than a technical exercise.

Very occasionally, buildings are 'spot-listed', an instant form of protection that usually occurs when design proposals are fairly advanced. In such cases the recognition of the building comes not from the immediate community, but from a more geographically remote group of architectural experts who deem it worthy of protection. The Urban and Regional Studies building at Reading University, designed by HKPA architects in the early 1970s, is an example: its spot-listing in 2016, just before Hawkins\Brown submitted for planning, has led to a redesign, further respecting the building's 'special features' while providing a creative and sustainable environment for its future occupants, as the client's original brief required. At the time of writing, the building sits cold and dark while the ideas of various groups about what is important are argued out – hopefully not for too long. It is the background buildings, not those that are celebrated and 'listed', that are particularly tricky; they do not come with a description of special architectural features and an acknowledgement that they are important to people.

To adapt any building is to be mindful of all this, thinking beyond the bricks and mortar to the impact it has on its occupants, the local community and its wider admirers. It is important to ask how all this will affect the client's aspirations, and whether the societal value of the reuse is being considered alongside the financial.

When we design new buildings from scratch, we can generally satisfy the brief's basic requirements, such as floor areas and room adjacencies. But when we embark on a refurbishment, we often have little idea of how the building will challenge, shock or delight before we start peeling back the layers, so it can

be a reactive rather than a proactive process. The pressure of money and programme means that design teams progress in haste, and the client maintains a risk register and a contingency fund to cover unknowns; the trouble is that 'unknowns' are by their nature difficult to quantify. For instance, over the years we have discovered that the 'Victorian' building at the Roald Dahl Museum in Buckinghamshire was actually much older; and that almost all the 1,000 or so concrete openings at Park Hill were different; and we have uncovered Anglo-Saxon loom weights in a basement on James Street in Covent Garden.

It is these moments of serendipity and the process of getting 'under the skin' of existing buildings that render them a rich source of creativity. We learned about the history of 'Elephant House' in Camden, north London, a dilapidated Victorian warehouse that was part of the Elephant Pale Ale Brewery. Then we found one of the original bottle caps buried on the site; it has since been subtly planted into the entrance door so that those in the know can proudly recall their building's history.

Opportunities do not always come through the uncovering of historic artefacts, however. The Broadcast Centre at Here East (see pages 39–49) was built with a 240-metre-long quadruple-height steel frame (or gantry) along one of its facades, with the intention of supporting ventilation units for the studios inside the building. The brief sought to demolish the gantry, until the idea of retaining it as a frame on which to stack small, individual studio units was sparked. The concept grew from an interest in Renaissance 'cabinets of curiosities'; here was one at an epic scale. This opened the floodgates to a plethora of ideas about how it could be

It's Not Just a Refurb

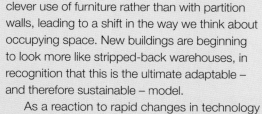

used. The common thread was that it would be affordable and – given its proximity to Hackney Wick, which has the highest concentration of artists' studios in Europe – occupied by creative people. Building at a small scale to populate the gantry provided the opportunity to reflect on the industrial heritage of the site, and previous occupiers Matchbox Cars and London Cure smoked salmon, among others, are referenced in the design of the units. This is an example of a *brief* evolving to fit the *building* – and the result is a solution that would never have been conceived as a new-build.

The desire for a connection with the past is deeply rooted in the human psyche. We seek authenticity, and that is often lost when buildings are adapted. It's a difficult balance to achieve, and we don't always get it right. We research, listen and learn as we design; it is an iterative process and requires an open mind and lateral thinking, not just from us but also from our clients. As a friend of mine once put it, old buildings bite back!

In addition to the societal and financial value of reusing buildings, it is the value to the environment that provides the most universally accepted argument for adaptation over demolition. One of the focuses of *WRK:LDN: Shaping London's Future Workplaces* (2016), an insight study by the independent built-environment organization New London Architecture into innovative workplace design, was the provision of adaptable buildings to ensure the future resilience of the city. The report found that the 'reuse of older buildings is in line with a greater emphasis on sustainability and a longer-term vision, while their heritage adds character that can align with and enhance the

[occupying] company's image and identity.'

Robust structures with generous floor-to-ceiling heights and large windows are inherently adaptable; the popularity of buildings from the late nineteenth and early twentieth centuries is testament to that. Metropolitan Wharf on the north bank of the River Thames in London is now on its third life, as a mix of studios, offices and high-end loft apartments, and it will no doubt evolve again in years to come.

Increasingly, buildings are being stripped back to their structural frame, and holes knocked through slabs to provide vertical connections between floors. This encourages collaboration among the occupants, and the subsequent cross-fertilization of ideas – all good ingredients for innovation and creative thinking. More intimate spaces are now being created through the

clever use of furniture rather than with partition walls, leading to a shift in the way we think about occupying space. New buildings are beginning to look more like stripped-back warehouses, in recognition that this is the ultimate adaptable – and therefore sustainable – model.

As a reaction to rapid changes in technology and swathes of new development, people value more than ever a connection to the past. 'Authenticity' is a word that springs up regularly in discussions about our built environment, probably because so much of what is built feels contrived. To arrive at a creative solution to the reuse of a building, we must cast the net wide, considering the impact on the local community and culture, the environment, the building's possible future and its uncertain past. It's a battle, but one that is well worth fighting.

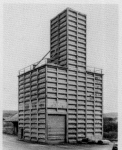

The St John's Hill Estate in Battersea, southwest London, was a fortress-like enclave of deteriorating 1930s flats. Its replacement is a scheme that knits itself back into the Victorian townscape with buildings of individual character and open, welcoming spaces.

In 1936, when the Peabody Trust – one of London's oldest and largest housing associations – welcomed its first tenants to the estate, the development was seen as the last word in modern social housing. A strong sense of community quickly took root. Street parties were common, and when war came and residents joined the campaign to 'Dig for Victory', the main square was given over to vegetable plots.

That community spirit, which extended to the surrounding terraced streets, had long since evaporated when Peabody decided to implement an ambitious plan to rebuild the estate. A labyrinthine layout and the high surrounding wall had made the development a no-go zone for outsiders. The social divisions grew ever wider as property prices in Battersea rose and single, upwardly mobile city workers replaced families who had been rooted in the area for decades. Problems caused by the foreboding isolation of the estate were matched by the poor state of the flats, which had long suffered from damp and condensation, high heating bills and the consequences of poor alterations to room layouts made when bathrooms replaced the original communal washrooms.

Opposite One of four new brick relief artworks by the artist Rodney Harris that tie the new development to its residents' past.

Below Plot 1 of the new development, which sits next to an Edwardian terrace, is similar in scale to the older houses, with a tonally complementary brick facade.

More, bigger, better homes

Peabody wanted to wipe the slate clean and create new, modern homes and an estate that felt part of the community again – one that reconnected with the surrounding street pattern and encouraged locals into and through its central shared space. To keep the existing community intact, the Trust would rehouse every resident who wanted to return, at the same tenure, while adding new private homes for sale to help subsidize the scheme.

The association asked Hawkins\Brown to design a scheme that could realize its vision of 'a new piece of London', and in so doing create a new template for the city's social housing. The architects responded with a masterplan of several buildings that together would deliver not just new, improved homes but also bigger ones, and 50 per cent more of them. By making better use of the site and increasing the footprint of buildings, it was possible to fit in nearly 600 homes relatively comfortably, in place of the previous 353.

With the close cooperation of the residents' steering group, Hawkins\Brown developed living spaces that could adapt to the changing demands of modern domestic life. All homes would enjoy their own private balconies or gardens, and access to landscaped public spaces, a wild garden, a play area and a central open square with a new community centre, as well as more than 500 square metres of ground-floor retail and commercial space. The buildings would be completed over three phases of demolition and reconstruction, and the process of decanting existing residents would be managed carefully, so that most would need to move only once.

Walls that welcome, not divide

The experience of living on the estate – which has been renamed Burridge Gardens – will be transformed. Hawkins\Brown's design removes the notorious perimeter wall and stitches the scheme into the environment surrounding it. The practice assigned a different design team to each building, so that within the overall scheme individual architectural visions could be expressed that reflected their context.

For example, one of the buildings in the first phase sits next to an Edwardian terrace and church, and consists of traditional-style town houses with front and back gardens and rusticated brickwork. Within the main body of the scheme, the design is more contemporary. To the west, the block overlooking busy railway lines running into Clapham

Peabody Burridge Gardens

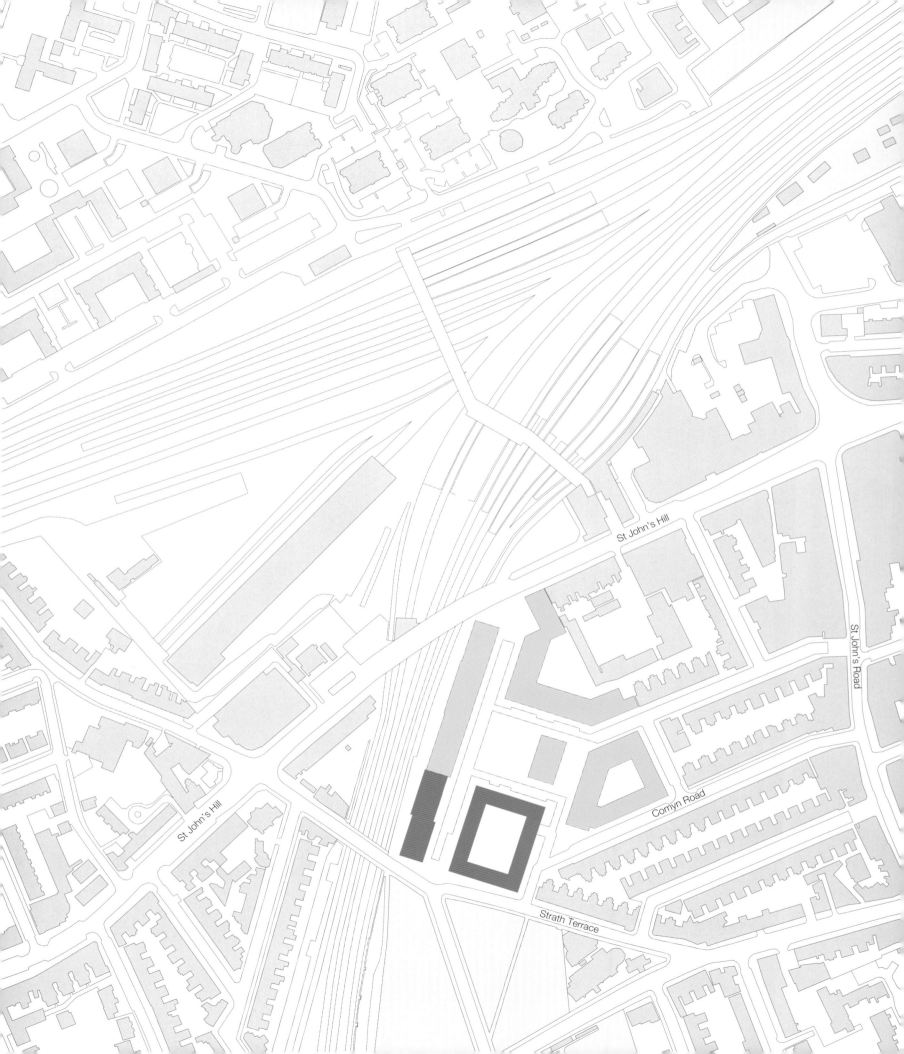

St John's Hill

St John's Hill

St John's Road

Comyn Road

Strath Terrace

Junction station acts as an acoustic buffer, reducing noise in the estate dramatically and improving the quality of Burridge Gardens' open spaces. Acoustic attenuation panels in the flats facing the railway keep noise out while letting in air, ventilating homes naturally as if through an open window.

By way of great contrast with the repeated, monotonous design of the original blocks, the new design gives each building its own identity, with a distinctive style and detailing, while retaining common threads that make each new block feel part of a whole. The use of brick throughout binds the scheme together, but the variety of different stocks creates character and breaks down the scale of the development, from the dark engineering brick of the railway-side block to handmade biscuit- and cream-coloured bricks to the south. Sandblasted into the brick of several of the facades are relief sculptures by the sculptor Rodney Harris. Hawkins\Brown's collaboration with Harris has led to artworks that recall the estate's history and residents' memories through domestic objects such as clothes, tools and a washroom sink. If all seems new around here, these sculptures offer continuity with the past.

Showing the way

The rich diversity of the buildings, heightened by the brightly hued glossy tiles that mark their entrances, is designed to generate identity and visual interest, but it also helps with wayfinding, offering clear signals to anyone who is unsure of their bearings. The scheme itself serves as an invitation to non-residents to start treating Burridge Gardens as a place that welcomes them, too. The tree-lined pedestrian boulevard that crosses the site and its connections with other streets open up new walking routes to and from Clapham Junction for commuters. At the station end, a new public square with commercial units extends the 'high street' of St John's Hill into the scheme.

The streets of the development have been laid out with level kerbs, creating a shared surface that encourages their use as social, pedestrian spaces. At the heart of Burridge Gardens, the main square's mature trees, plants, street furniture and community hub – the Portakabin beloved of the former estate, transformed into an architectural centrepiece – create a space that is inviting, safe and congenial for the families who have homes here, as well as for the wider community. In consigning the St John's Hill fortress to the past, Burridge Gardens shows the way for the future of social housing in London.

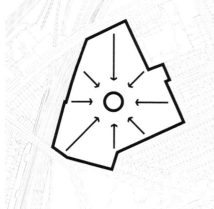

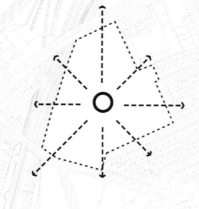

Opposite Site plan showing the completed Phase 1, with future phases highlighted.

Top A model created for community consultations shows Hawkins\Brown's full masterplan.

Above, from left The original estate looked inwards; the future outward-looking neighbourhood removes boundaries.

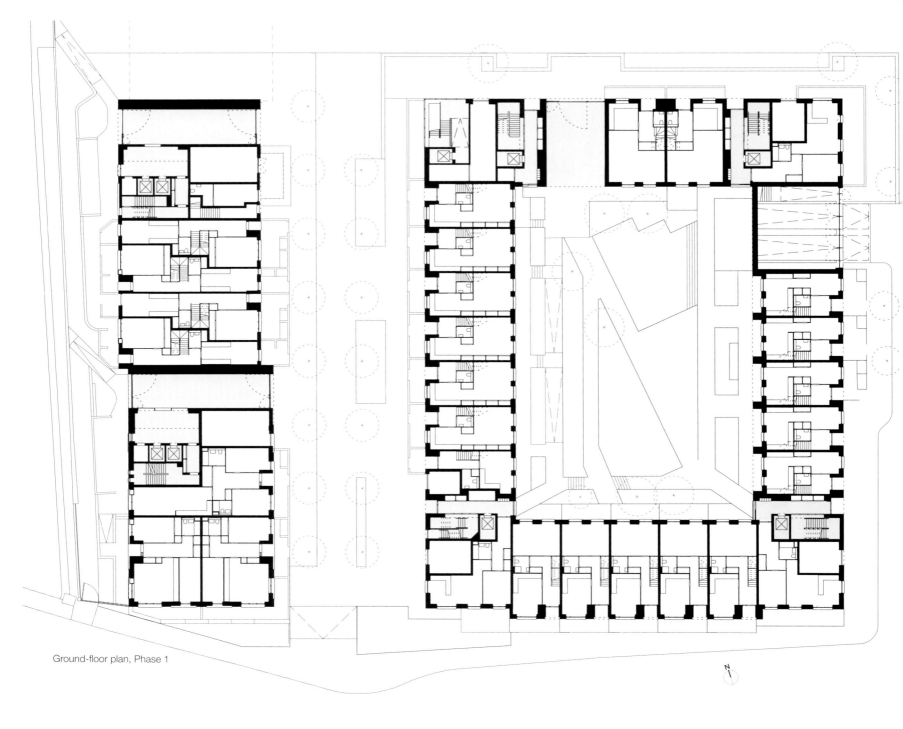

Ground-floor plan, Phase 1

PROJECT DATA

LOCATION
Wandsworth, London

CLIENT
Peabody

SIZE
17,275 square metres

START DATE
2007

COMPLETION DATE
2016 (Phase 1)

Opposite, bottom West–east section, Phase 1: from the railway cutting in the west to the Edwardian conservation area in the east.

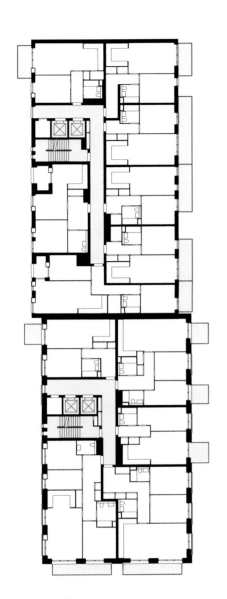

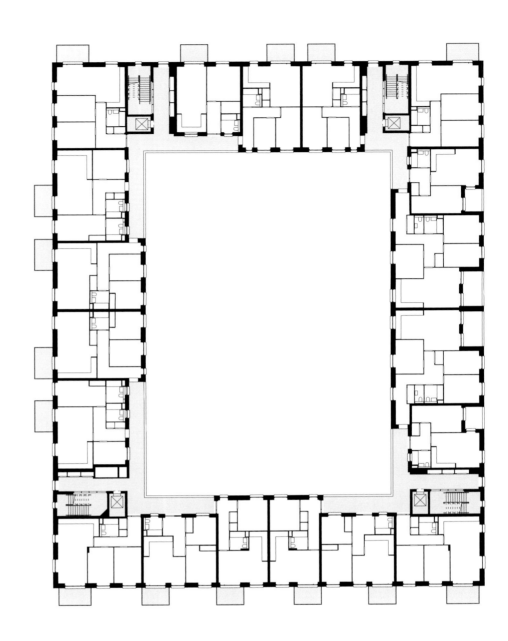

Upper-floor plan, Phase 1

Opposite The new buildings next to the railway cutting are designed as an acoustic, reducing noise from passing trains and improving the quality of the public realm.

Below A new pedestrian avenue crosses the previously cut-off site, welcoming in the wider community and creating a direct connection between Clapham Junction station and Wandsworth Common.

Each unique brick building has its own identity. Communal entrances are highlighted with coloured glazed brick, a simple wayfinding device for visitors.

A pineapple pattern – a symbol of welcome inspired by decorative carving found on the original site – is used on the entrance gates, neatly symbolizing the transformation of the estate.

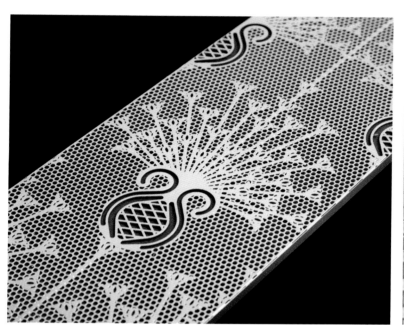

Above The new Burridge Gardens offers residents more spacious homes and high-quality landscaped communal and public spaces to enjoy.

Right The buildings are positioned to create legible streets with well-defined pedestrian and trafficked areas, and many ground-level homes are accessed directly from the street.

Right Acoustic vent panels are a novel inclusion for a residential development, and offer a sustainable, cost-effective alternative to air-conditioning while blocking out sound.

Below The new development opens up the estate and increases the density and mix of homes without losing the sense of place and community.

Overleaf A visualization of the next two phases, which will involve the construction of more than 445 homes, a community centre, commercial and retail space, and a public square.

Hawkins\Brown have been working at Tottenham Court Road in central London for more than twenty-five years. Their recent upgrade of the Underground station, culminating in vibrant new entrances, has created a much-expanded ticket hall and below-ground station. Their work on the station's Elizabeth line, meanwhile – the jewel in the Crossrail crown – is reshaping not only the city's infrastructure but also the experience of the people who use it every day.

More than a machine

The thing about infrastructure is that it just works. It's only when there's a glitch or failure that we, the people who rely on it, are reminded that it is in fact our support system and helps to define our lives: getting us from A to B, taking us from work to play, and leading us back to our families.

Hawkins\Brown know how to make infrastructure work. They know how to tame the massively complex engineering and design requirements while keeping a station operational. But, more than that, they understand that these projects have a responsibility to integrate themselves into the city, improving the public realm and covering over the scars of construction, all while enhancing the human experience. And that last aspect is where Hawkins\Brown excels.

About 150,000 people currently use Tottenham Court Road station every day, and that figure is expected to rise to 200,000 when services begin on the Elizabeth line in 2018. The concept for the station was to make sure that it would act as one transport interchange, creating seamless connections between Underground lines and Crossrail with accessibility for all.

The upgrade at Tottenham Court Road has massively improved the comfort of travellers who had once fought their way through the cramped ticket hall, duelling for escalator space. As well as an expanded ticket hall – it is six times larger – there are new entrances to all sides of St Giles Circus, more escalators, and improved passageways and platforms. The public realm has also been upgraded with the creation of new public plazas at the foot of the Centre Point tower. Not only that, the station is chock-full of art.

Art for everyone

You'll find everyone in the Underground. It is a truly democratic place that almost everyone who comes into London passes through. And although everyone might be weaving through the same spaces, each person experiences them in different ways. Tottenham Court Road station has ten times the audience of Tate Modern. So why not give those people something to think about?

Art in the Underground isn't new, certainly not at Tottenham Court Road station, where Eduardo Paolozzi's glass mosaic of urban industrial scenes winds through the Northern and Central line platforms and an array of interconnecting spaces. Hawkins\Brown have continued in this tradition, working with the French artist Daniel Buren to create an artwork that befits the station while complementing Paolozzi's sprawling masterpiece. Some 95 per cent of Paolozzi's original tiles remain, now restored and cleaned, but some – the arched entrance pieces – were removed and are to be displayed at Paolozzi's alma mater, the University of Edinburgh. Buren, known for his Op art-style geometric shapes and stripes, collaborated with Hawkins\Brown for more than a decade to realize *Diamonds and Circles*, a permanent *in situ* artwork brought to life by the movement of people through the station. The Underground entrances are marked by the colours of the circles and diamonds: monochrome for the Oxford Street side and vibrant hues for the plaza entrances at the base of Centre Point.

Opposite Passengers pass Daniel Buren's permanent artwork *The Big Wall, Up and Down, Diamonds and Circles, Blue, Green, Orange, Red, Yellow* at the Charing Cross Road exit of the station, commissioned in collaboration with Art on the Underground.

Right An early sketch by Buren, showing what would become the ticket hall vitrine component, *In the Window, Diamond and Circle, Blue and Yellow*.

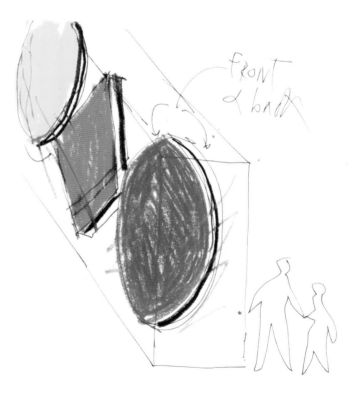

Tottenham Court Road Station

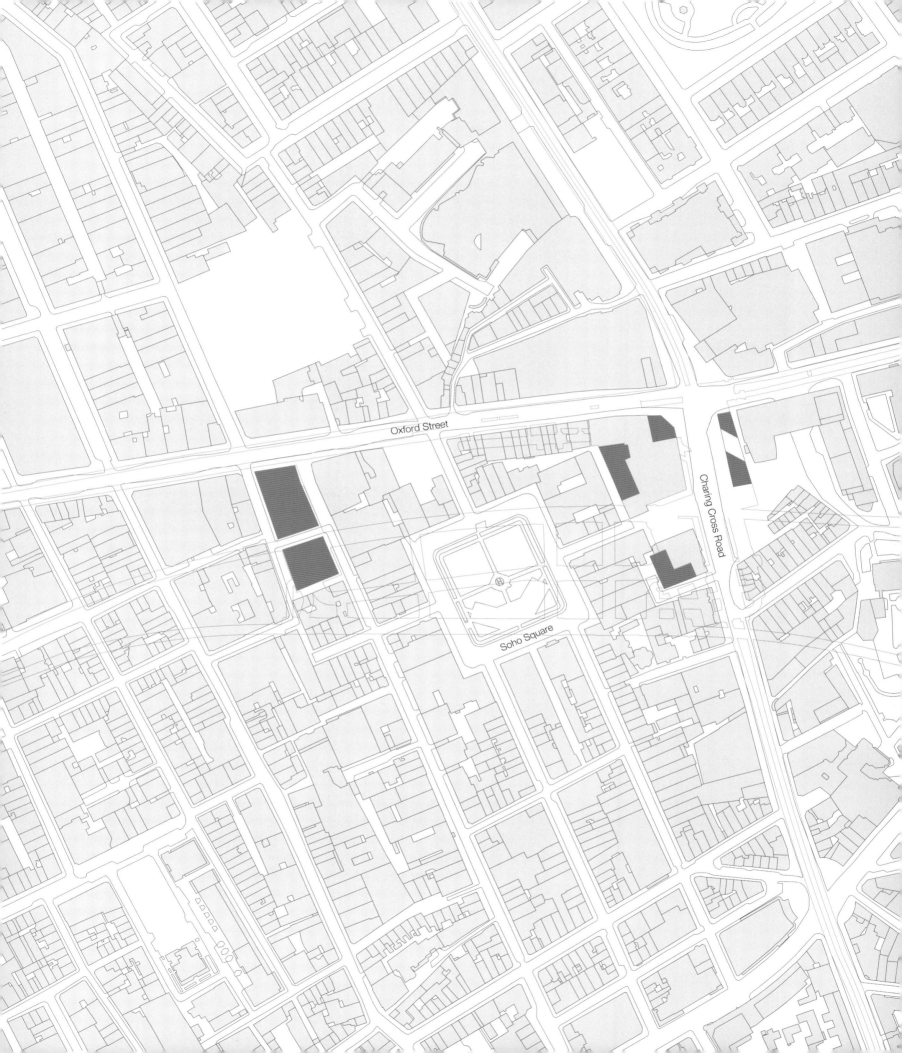

Oxford Street

Charing Cross Road

Soho Square

Full steam ahead

From Paolozzi to Buren, the rich history of art at Tottenham Court Road continues with the new Crossrail development. A new western entrance and ticket hall by Hawkins\Brown will be completed in 2018, and an over-site development is being designed.

Each entrance to the station has a distinctive character that reflects the environment and heritage of its particular neighbourhood. This also makes it easier for tourists and everyday users to find their way around. The station serves two of London's most energetic districts: St Giles and Soho. At St Giles, the Underground ticket hall links to the eastern entrance of the Elizabeth line with Buren's bold shapes, which reflect the 1960s iconography of Centre Point. Another commission, by the Turner Prize-winning artist Richard Wright, gilds the ceiling of one of the eastern escalator boxes in gold leaf.

The new western ticket hall at Dean Street, by contrast, is dark, cinematic and redolent of Soho itself, and the art here is a twist on the neighbourhood's nocturnal tilt. With *Exquisite Corpse* by Douglas Gordon, another Turner Prize-winner, passengers encounter a series of screens displaying images that invoke the history, culture and character of Soho.

Another identifier for Tottenham Court Road station are the 'drum' light fittings that contrast with the station's concrete structure. These fittings, designed by Hawkins\Brown, appear to float through the space in both the eastern and western ticket halls and incorporate lighting, acoustic attenuation and station communications systems.

Hawkins\Brown's work at Tottenham Court Road is a lesson in how infrastructure should be. It should serve people as easily and seamlessly as possible, but, more than that, it should make the journey itself more interesting.

Opposite The site plan shows the underground and above-ground developments of Tottenham Court Road London Underground and Elizabeth line stations.

This page A visualization and construction photograph of the exposed concrete ceilings, bespoke lighting and acoustic drums at the Elizabeth line Soho ticket hall.

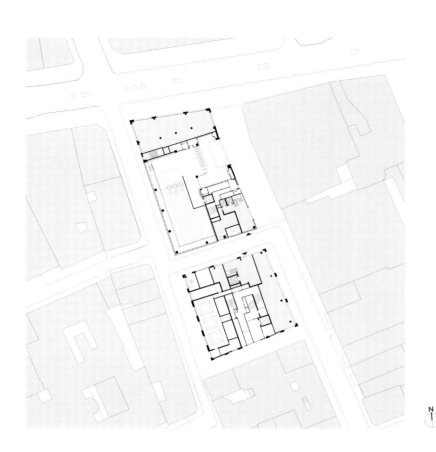

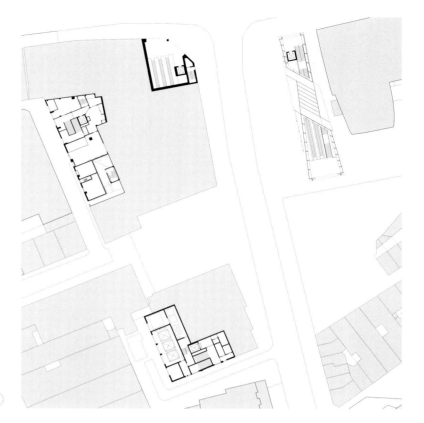

N

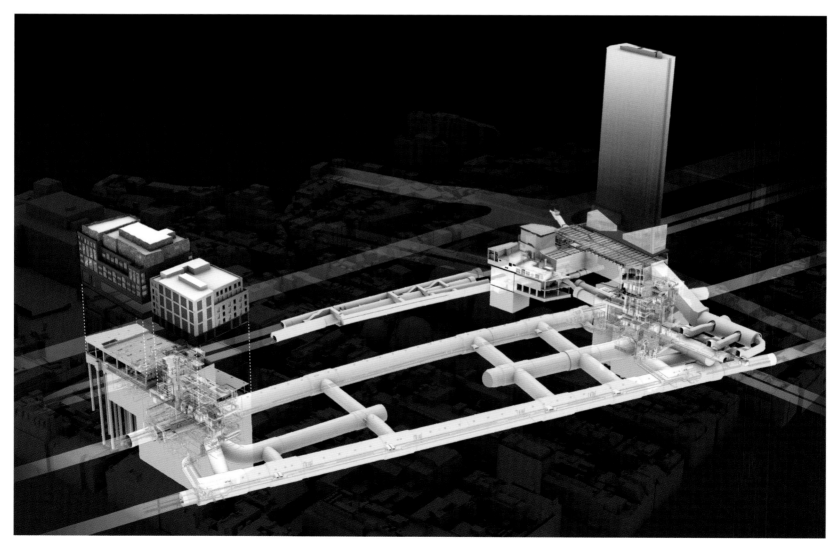

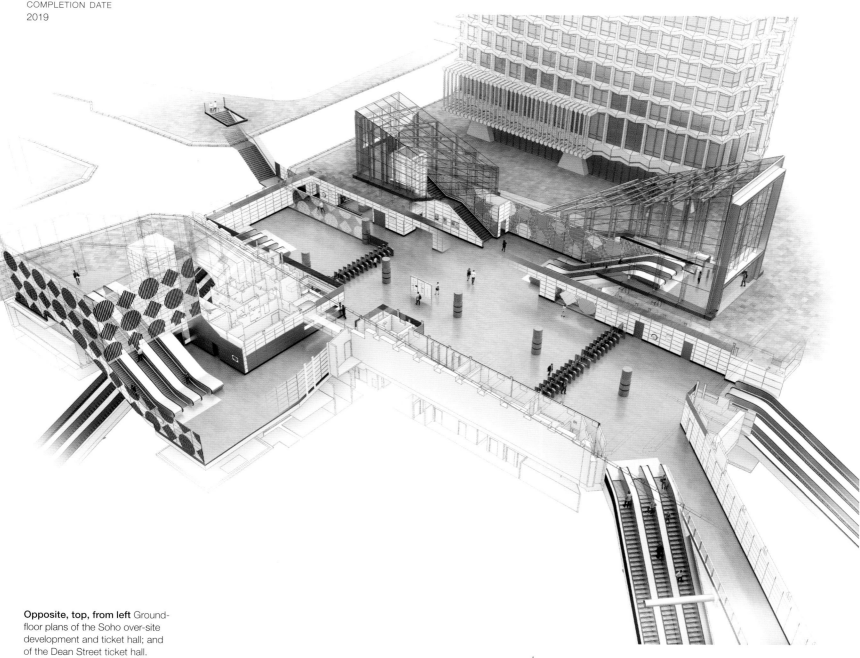

PROJECT DATA

LOCATION
Fitzrovia, London

CLIENT
London Underground; Crossrail

SIZE
5 hectares

START DATE
early 1990s

COMPLETION DATE
2019

Opposite, top, from left Ground-floor plans of the Soho over-site development and ticket hall; and of the Dean Street ticket hall.

Opposite, bottom Axonometric view of the new Elizabeth line station, platforms, over-site development and how it stitches into the Dean Street ticket hall (on the left).

Above Illustration of the upgraded London Underground ticket hall linking to the eastern entrance of the Elizabeth line.

Tottenham Court Road London Underground station under construction (top) and the Elizabeth line tunnelling demonstrate the scale of the project.

A visualization of the Soho oversite development, with ornamental panels based on the etched glass windows of a pub that once stood on a nearby corner.

Eduardo Paolozzi's mosaics
from 1986, now renovated,
reflect the artist's interpretation
of the local area and his interest
in mechanization, urbanization,
popular culture and everyday life.

Daniel Buren's black-and-white artwork *The Big Wall, Up and Down, Diamonds and Circles, Black and White* acts as wayfinding, signifying the Oxford Street entrance to the Dean Street ticket hall.

Morag Morrison

There are clear parallels in the way architecture and art have developed in the United Kingdom since the late 1980s. The tendency has been to move away from the self-centred products of the 'starchitect', with each work pursuing his or her individual style, and from what many people see as the self-obsessed artwork on a plinth in the white cube of the art gallery. Both disciplines have become far more open to new knowledge and insights from others, whether they be clients, users, fellow designers or artists, engineers or contractors. At Hawkins\Brown we see the value of working together on an interdisciplinary adventure without limits, and this has become fundamental to our practice.

The summer of 1988 – which brought the end of the Thatcherite boom – was a turning point for many. It was a time of optimism and opportunity for Generation X. Michael Craig-Martin described his art students at Goldsmiths (now part of University of London) as 'a combination of youthful bravado, innocence, fortunate timing, good luck and of course good work'.

When those students, led by Damien Hirst, put together their own exhibition in a disused London Port Authority building, the event marked the start of a renaissance in British art and the birth of the Young British Artist. The exhibition was entitled *Freeze* after a photograph by Matt Collishaw of the moment a bullet hits a skull. The successful show was publicized widely, and as a result the careers of all sixteen featured artists took off. The economic climate of the time meant that there were plenty of empty shops and warehouses in which they could show their work, and a new generation of wealthy collectors, including Charles Saatchi, helped to create a much wider audience for their work.

Artists – like architects – became more sociable and more enterprising.

Those two words could also be applied to Russell Brown and Roger Hawkins as they walked out of Rock Townsend to set up Hawkins\Brown. As artists gained the confidence and acceptance to work outside the institution and engage with much wider audiences, architecture at Hawkins\Brown began to engage directly with these artists. In the 1990s this manifested itself in projects for Crossrail, the then Birmingham Institute of Art & Design and the Arts Council at Gillett Square in London, working with the artists Peter Doig, Richard Wilson, Nicky Hirst and Andrew Cross.

Hawkins\Brown could see that working with artists brought a richness and poignancy that complemented their architecture. This can be seen in such projects as 'Salt Bridges', where four artists (Nicky Hirst, Annie Cattrell, Tim Head and Peter Fraser) collaborated with us and the Department of Biochemistry at the University of Oxford to create artworks for the new building. The six site-specific pieces that ultimately made their way into the atrium of the building were symbolic of a three-year collaboration that explored the research of the scientists, the design process of Hawkins\Brown and the construction process of Laing O'Rourke. The very fact of running an arts programme in Oxford brought many benefits to the project: it gave the scientists the confidence to discuss aesthetics, which facilitated discussions about the design of their new building; it helped the biochemists to create a stronger visual language for publishing their research papers; and, most importantly, it created a strong identity for the department, encouraging more students to apply to biochemistry courses.

Meanwhile, across the Channel, the French artist Daniel Buren had long been challenging the relationship of the visual arts with their place of presentation. With his trademark 8.7-centimetre-wide black and coloured stripes, he had moved away from creating paintings and started to make site-specific installations, such as *Les Deux Plateaux* in the courtyard of the Palais Royal in Paris, and had adorned the streets of Paris and New York with his work. In 2007 he was selected by Transport for London (TfL) and Art on the Underground for a large commission to enhance the visitor's experience at Tottenham Court Road Tube station. He was the natural choice to create a piece that would complement the refurbished Eduardo Paolozzi mosaic murals at platform level.

With *Diamonds and Circles*, Buren organized the volumes of space that form the journey from the street to the ticket hall with a simple circle and diamond motif, and black stripes. He told me: 'I play with very simple forms that repeat themselves and change through the use of colour or not, and by the presence of the stripes, which are sometimes the form and sometimes the background.' The pattern is set out from the three-dimensional circle and diamond set in a vitrine in the centre of the ticket hall. It is a clever reference to the museum, and the fact that this work of art will be seen by far more visitors than any in a gallery in London. At 2.3 metres high – just over human scale – the circles and diamonds resonate with the commuters as they pass up and down the escalators.

Buren's work at the station helps to define the interior volumes and leads the visitor through them without the distraction of endless advertising posters or the usual London

Art and Architecture: Parallel Lines

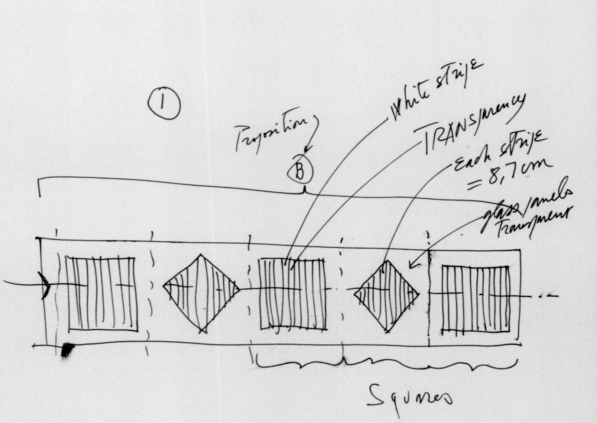

Underground paraphernalia. When I asked him how this commission had influenced his work, he told me that collaborating with Hawkins\Brown made him think more about how people navigate space and respond to visual stimuli. The great success of Buren's work for TfL at Tottenham Court Road station has given Crossrail the confidence to commission the artists Douglas Gordon and Richard Wright, with whom we are working to create site-specific works elsewhere in the station (see pages 105–15).

At a much smaller scale, but with a similar objective to Buren, Bridget Smith has been working with us on the Beecroft Building in Oxford (see pages 161–75). She is looking at changing a 30-metre stretch of facade at street level from a perforated screen to a 'window into the world of physics', showing light particles being refracted around the building. Her panels are handcrafted in the physics workshop using the same casting and drilling operations that the physicists use in constructing equipment for their experiments. While we worked on the project together, Smith told me that she finds beauty in such materiality and execution, and she uses this to create her dynamic light-beam pattern. As with Buren's work at Tottenham Court Road station, Smith's piece will engage the passer-by, this time through suggesting what activities are going on inside a building that cannot always be transparent.

Through working with artists, we have learned that architects have a natural tendency to try to solve problems, to find a rationale to resolve how a building should be designed and executed, how it should respond to a brief or to the people who inhabit it. Artists, on the other hand, don't try to solve the problem, but actively pose questions through their work. Their art is about how the

viewer experiences a piece or what that piece says about the world in which we live. A good example of this is Nicky Hirst's *Glass Menagerie* for the New Biochemistry building in Oxford (see page 161), where we were looking for a technical solution to reduce solar gain to the atrium and provide a stronger message about science practice. Hirst's work achieved this by applying Hermann Rorschach's famous ink-blot tests to the way we see and interpret science. When architects and artists come together and create a dialogue in a project, the result can be much more interesting, but both artist and architect must understand and respect the other's different approach.

All these projects show how collaborating with an artist can help a building, interior or landscape engage with a far wider audience than just its users. It can create a strong identity for the organization that inhabits it, but also, more importantly, it sets up a dialogue that can question, explain or intrigue. Workshops with

artists help both clients and architects to step back from the purely functional requirements of a building and address wider topics. We can see how the commuters at Tottenham Court Road have a little more spring in their step as they walk through Buren's *Diamonds and Circles*, and we have seen more collaborative research and a change in the visual representation of work from the biochemists at Oxford, thanks to the involvement of artists. In architectural terms, we are left with far richer buildings that go much further than just providing a background for art. They engage actively with the wider human questions that art can address.

A sketch by the artist Daniel Buren for his permanent installation *Diamonds and Circles* at Tottenham Court Road station.

Hackney Town Hall's art deco grandeur had long since faded when a major refurbishment was set in motion. Its restoration required the entire range of skills and specialisms, from reuse and repair to conversion and conservation.

When the doors of Hackney Town Hall opened for the first time in 1937, it was taken to the heart of this northeast London community as a symbol of civic pride, democracy and celebration. Designed by Lanchester & Lodge, it was a tour de force of art deco elegance. Marriages began in the most serene of surroundings; the business of local government enjoyed a stately backdrop, and its wheels were oiled by state-of-the-art building services.

In 1991 the architecture and interiors, still largely intact, earned the town hall a Grade II listing from English Heritage (now Historic England). But by the turn of the millennium the building was in a sorry state, having suffered years of underinvestment. Marble floor tiles were broken and missing, and wood panelling was peeling and badly discoloured. The seating in the Council Chamber was worn thin; the beautiful art deco chandeliers were missing glass panels and had been fitted with coloured bulbs; and building services were badly out of date. It was a wasteful, inefficient, sapping work environment for council employees and an unfit setting for deliberation, decision-making and administration affecting a quarter of a million Londoners.

Opposite Previously unused light wells have been converted into indoor event spaces featuring acoustic services walls with a digitally generated pattern that mimics the concealed brick facade.

Below The Town Hall's Portland stone facade has been cleaned, repaired and subtly upgraded. The original parapet hides new rooftop services set back from the edge.

No stone left unturned

In 2005 Hackney Council selected Hawkins\Brown to lead an all-encompassing restoration of the building. The aim was not only to return it to its original grandeur, but also to increase its staff capacity, modernize its IT, heating, ventilation and air-conditioning services, reduce waste and maximize the efficiency of both the building and its users.

Hawkins\Brown brought highly pertinent experience of updating town halls in nearby Stoke Newington and Barking & Dagenham, as well as personal experience as members of the local community: two of the practice's Partners, Russell Brown and Morag Morrison, were married there in 1992, and the pair registered the births of their children in the same rooms.

Extending the work over twelve years, through a complex series of overlapping phases linked to releases of funding, allowed the town hall to continue functioning throughout the project. Successful, sensitive collaboration was a hallmark throughout, among architect, consultants, contractors, specialist subconsultants and skilled craftspeople, in fields ranging from mechanical and electrical engineering to audio-visual systems, joinery and French polishing. All work had to be meticulously directed and coordinated by the team of designers at Hawkins\Brown.

Making eighty years disappear

Working with the existing building fabric and weaving in new services required the full spectrum of intervention. Two unused, abandoned light wells at the heart of the building were converted into bright, airy, multifunctional indoor event spaces with the addition of ETFE (ethylene tetrafluoroethylene) roofs and raised floors. New services and IT were threaded through original ducts, corridors and service openings wherever possible to prevent the new from intruding on the old. Where entire rooms were repurposed to create new spaces, such as the 1930s-style bar, they were fashioned with fittings and lighting that echoed the original designs and materials. Outside, the Portland stone elevations were cleaned and repaired.

From the grand facade to the stitching on seats, the project demanded attention to detail at every scale. A team of dedicated master craftspeople worked on rescuing the interiors. Chandeliers and light fittings were refurbished and updated with modern sources, and new fittings fabricated in the spirit of the originals. Timber panelling in the Council Chamber and other official rooms required meticulous restoration by skilled French polishers. Original floor tiles

Hackney Town Hall

Graham Road

Morning Lane

Mare Street

Richmond Road

in rare Swedish green marble had to be sliced in half painstakingly slowly – taking ten hours per tile – to create replacements for broken ones. New seating in the Council Chamber and elsewhere was fabricated with wooden frames and upholstery to match the 1930s designs. More than 300 original Crittall windows were removed to a workshop, stripped, repaired and upgraded with ultra-slim double glazing before being painted and refitted.

A twenty-first-century town hall

The building now looks as good as new. But, just as importantly, it functions better and more sustainably than it ever did. The decision to restore rather than rebuild avoided the embodied carbon cost of a new building, and the architectural interventions, materials and building services focused on reducing waste and extending the lifespan and efficiency of the building. The installation of photovoltaic panels and a combined heat and power

Highly skilled and, wherever possible, local craftspeople were commissioned for the painstaking restoration of the interiors.

system has helped to halve the energy use and carbon footprint for each employee.

No longer is the building prolifically leaking heat. The roofing-over of the light wells with ETFE reduced the energy needed to heat the adjacent spaces, and ultra-slim, low-emissivity, double-glazed units in the refurbished Crittall windows cut heat loss there dramatically. Low-energy measures include the adaptation of original light fittings to incorporate high-efficiency dimmable fluorescent or LED sources, and the installation of efficient condensing boilers.

Hawkins\Brown's space planning of the office areas resulted in a two-thirds increase in staff capacity. Rooms standing idle were put to use, and new spaces were created within the original footprint, including kitchens for events and a council print shop.

This being a major public building and the revitalized symbol of local government in a large inner-London borough, public accessibility was a vital element of the refurbishment. A careful balance had to be struck between the interests of conservation and accessibility, taking into account the United Kingdom's disability access legislation, building regulations and the views of English Heritage. Four new passenger lifts, two of them in the newly created atriums, made a dramatic difference, and involved only minimal disturbance to the existing building fabric. The third new lift provides access from the ground floor to the Assembly Halls, which could previously be reached only by the Grand Staircase; and the fourth connects the public with the Committee Rooms and Council Chamber, and staff with offices and training rooms.

An investment for the borough

Working in partnership with Hackney Council, English Heritage, the Hackney Conservation Department and a host of specialist consultants and contractors, Hawkins\Brown have brought a much-loved civic landmark back to life. The revival has given back to the people of Hackney a centre they can be proud of – a treasure of art deco architecture and design in which to celebrate the most important events of their lives.

Council employees now enjoy a workplace that is comfortable, superbly equipped and easy to move about in. And the council has a more productive, more dignified town hall with the capacity to generate valuable income for years to come – funds to invest in the borough and to bring the best possible services to its residents.

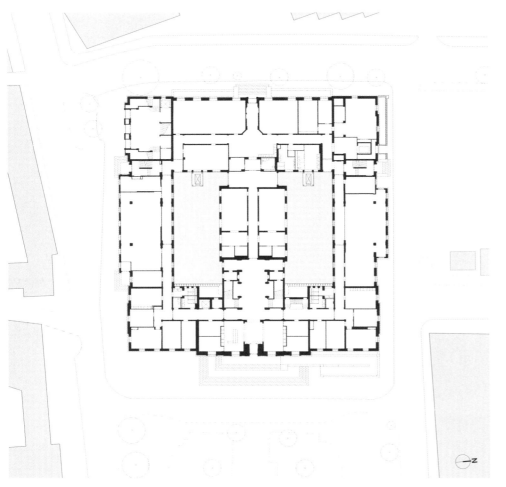

Ground-floor plan

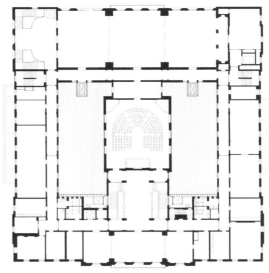

Upper-floor plan

A section shows the Council Chamber at the heart of the building, accessible from the public entrance.

PROJECT DATA

LOCATION
Hackney, London

CLIENT
London Borough of Hackney

SIZE
11,500 square metres

START DATE
2005

COMPLETION DATE
2017

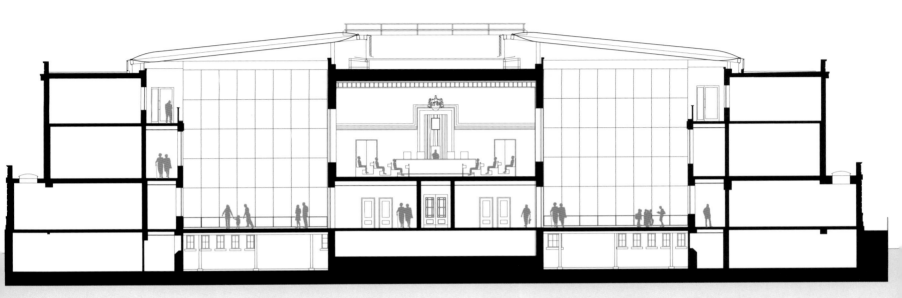

Traditional, rare French polishing methods were used to renovate the largely unaltered timber-panelled rooms, including the Council Chamber, committee rooms and the speaker's parlour.

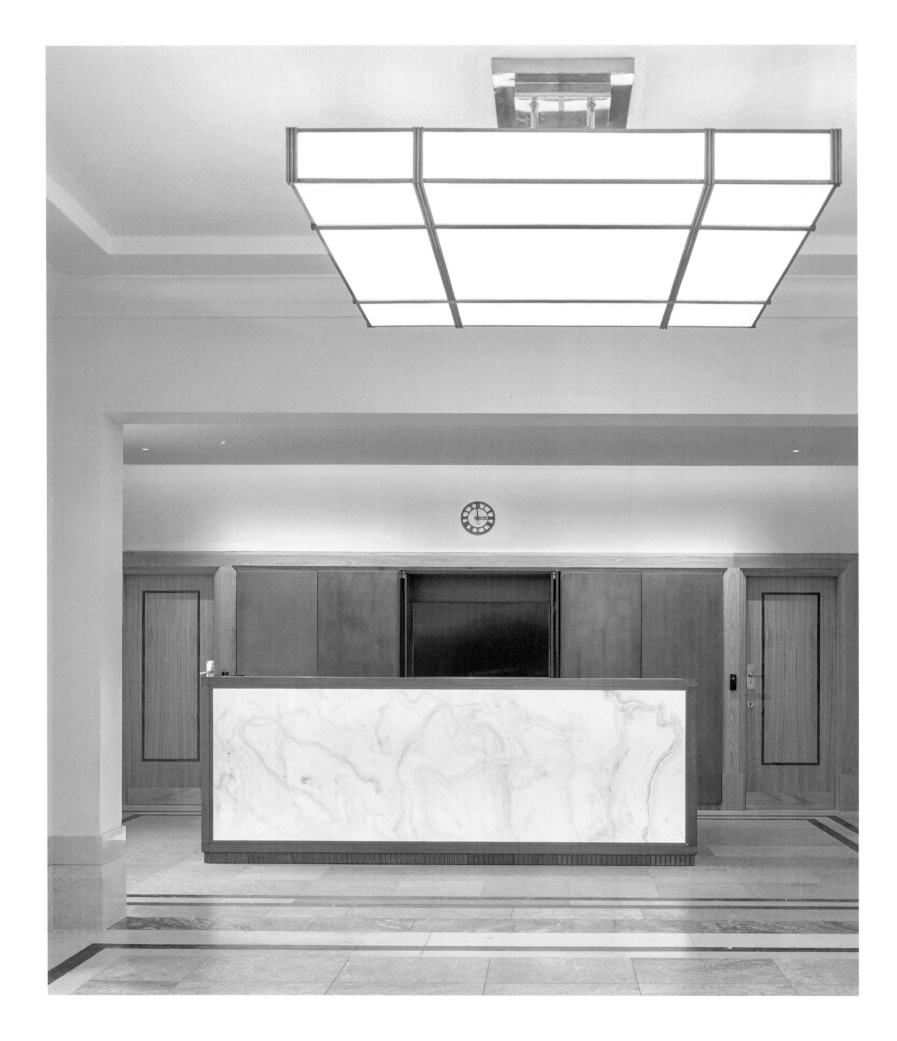

The elegant Bridgetown Bar was one of the first spaces to be completed, in 2012, with a contemporary art deco-style interior design.

Opposite In the reception area the original palette of bronze, marble, walnut and oak is maintained, and all the new elements take inspiration from the restored art deco features.

Details of the newly restored
marble and resin terrazzo floors
throughout respect the originals
from 1937.

The reception and public areas are more open, brighter and fully accessible, with new finishes that blend in with those of the restored original.

The beautiful original light fittings were restored, altered and converted to modern sources, and new fittings were designed to match the originals.

Natural light floods the building through the restored Crittall windows, highlighting the quality of every detail.

So good to see a truly exemplary and wonderfully careful restoration of a great public building, making it fit for purpose as a twenty-first-century civic building and retaining the quality of the original.

DUNCAN WILSON, CHIEF EXECUTIVE, HISTORIC ENGLAND

This project was an exercise in creative ambiguity: the refurbishment of a Victorian warehouse and the construction of an extension whose design, materials and textures disguised its tender age. In the dense urban hotchpotch of ageing brick warehouses and newer buildings that dominates the area of London close to the River Thames, between Waterloo and London Bridge stations, 53 Great Suffolk Street was unremarkable. Built in the 1890s, the three-storey warehouse had housed a blacksmith's and a meatpacking factory, and was now home to architects and designers, while a single-storey extension at the side of the building was being used as a car park.

The location, though, suggested untapped potential. With two major rail termini within ten minutes' walk and Southwark Tube station just a few moments away, the site was well connected for public transport and could benefit from the wave of positive sentiment spreading through the local property market after the regeneration of the riverbank around Tate Modern. As it was, the building hardly made the most of its site.

Hawkins\Brown were appointed by the building's owner at the time to explore the residential, commercial and mixed-use alternatives for developing the property. Commercial won out, and it was decided that replacing the car park lean-to with an extension of similar volume and form to the existing warehouse, and creating a unified, high-quality, flexible, distinctive workspace across the two structures, would create a more valuable asset with a strong appeal to creative businesses.

The existing building already had a great deal going for it. Inside, raw, exposed brick walls, concrete beams and columns helped to make it a compelling workspace. These features would simply be repaired and cleaned, and would provide the basis for the palette of materials to be used in the new areas, with internal walls built in solid brick and painted white, and ceilings of exposed concrete. The steel frame of the older building had been encased in concrete to fireproof it; the new building's steel columns would be left exposed and painted with intumescent paint.

Brick, concrete and steel

Truth to materials and an avoidance of artifice became the defining themes of the project, both inside and out. Neither plasterboard nor wallpaper would have a role anywhere in the scheme. This was to be a workspace enriched by the authentic, unadorned material language of construction – brick, concrete, steel, aluminium and little else.

The most striking application of this approach was the structure that would unify the warehouse and its extension. Stitching the floors of the two buildings together would be the centrepiece of the scheme: a cantilevered, raw-steel staircase with brass fittings, inside a glazed enclosure. Hawkins\Brown worked closely with a local specialist fabricator of steel staircases to achieve the intricate detailing of joints and weld locations, and perfect the waxing and buffing of the steel. A light well above the staircase draws daylight down into the heart of the building, and blown-glass light fittings complement the full-height glass enclosure. The raw steel is referenced throughout the scheme to tie old and new together.

To maximize the lettable office space, it was decided to insert a new top floor across both buildings. To achieve this without increasing the massing, within the envelope of the old warehouse, called for the introduction of continuous dormer windows at roof level. Structurally, it was less straightforward, since the foundations of the older building were too weak to support significantly more load. This led to the new floor in the warehouse being

Opposite The materials in the new reception area reference the building's industrial heritage.

Right A detail of the central staircase, in raw steel with brass fittings.

53 Great Suffolk Street

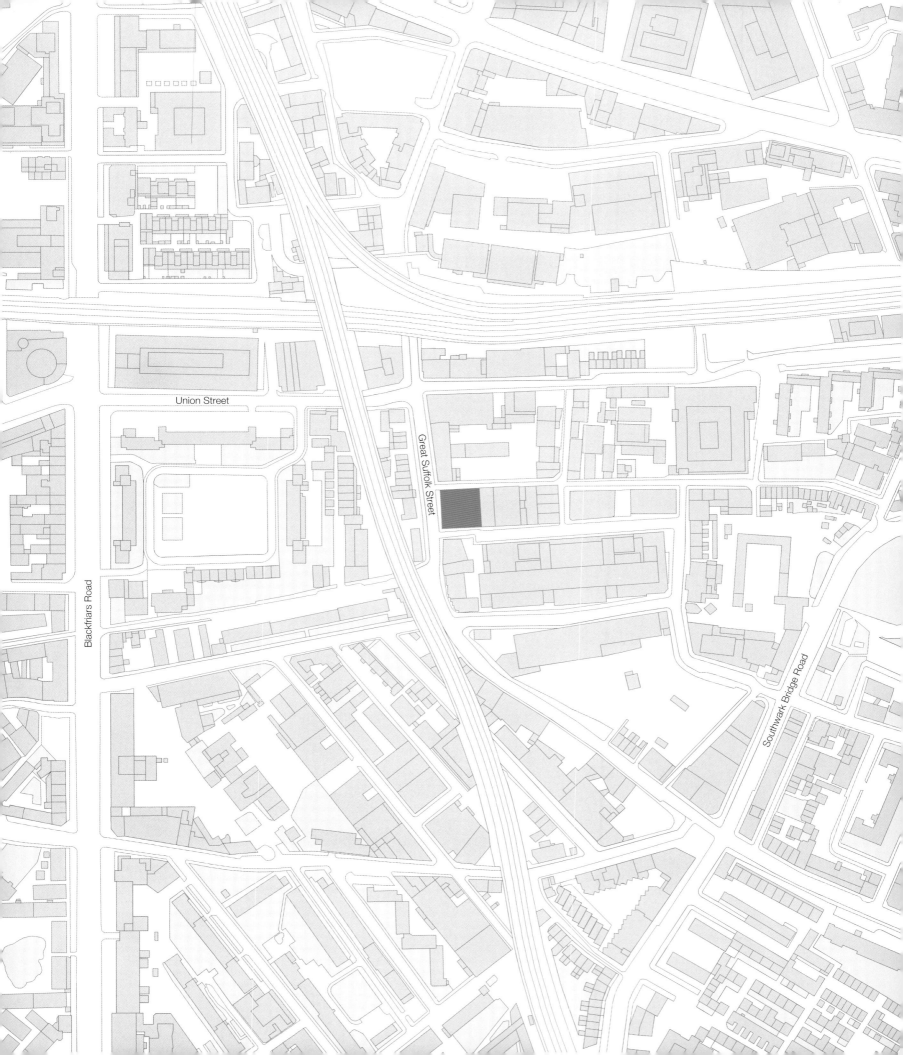

cantilevered, and its weight transferred to the foundations of the new building through four large steel beams, which run across the top floor at roof level.

A question of identity

The seamlessness between old and new that was achieved inside was less viable and less necessary on the outside, but also less desirable. Although the new building shares the scale and form of the warehouse, and its openings reference the position and orientation of the older structure's windows, the strategy in terms of materials would be to allow each building its own identity.

There would be no disguising the fact that, on the outside at least, these were two separate structures. Instead of trying to homogenize the whole scheme by sandblasting the brickwork of the older side into a fresh, clean expanse, the pitted, dirty London brick with its patchwork of infilled openings was left intact, to bear

witness to the passing of time and the many alterations carried out over the years.

The question was then how the new building should respond to its older sibling. The selection of external bricks would have a critical bearing on its identity, and so, early in the planning process, tests were carried out with a wide range of bricks, from a London stock that closely matched the warehouse to a deep purple variety. A light red waterstruck brick emerged as the initial frontrunner, and this was refined through site visits with the brick supplier.

One of these visits proved to be pivotal for the project, when the planning officer from the London Borough of Southwark, the local planning authority, joined the meeting and lent his support to a bolder, more varied, semi-glazed brick that had been proposed by Hawkins\Brown over the flatter red waterstrucks. A search followed to find a manufacturer that could supply the bricks to the required quality but in a relatively small run. The German bricks used in the scheme have a rich, varied surface colouring, the product of firing in one of the last traditional, coal-fired circular kilns in that country.

Affinity and ambiguity

Although this was the first time such bricks had been used in the United Kingdom, their irregular colouring and texture lend the new building a character that chimes with that of the surrounding Victorian red-brick buildings. The simultaneously sympathetic and unconventional dressing of the new-build, along with its traditional form and fenestration, make its age hard to read. It was this ambiguity, as well as the care and dialogue shown in the selection and sourcing of the bricks, that gained the scheme strong support from the borough.

Unlike so many recent additions to the Southwark streetscape, this building does not bark its presence and shiny newness. The new half makes no attempt to upstage the old, and the whole is content to strike up a conversation with its venerable neighbours. Importantly for its owners, it is a whole that doubles the gross floor area of the site, and constitutes a modern, crafted workplace of rare quality, exceptionally well-received by tenants, users, stakeholders and the local community.

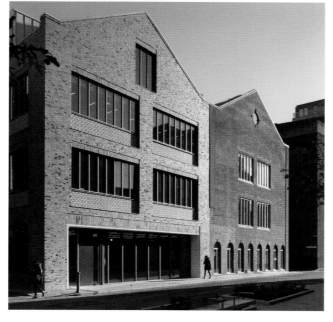

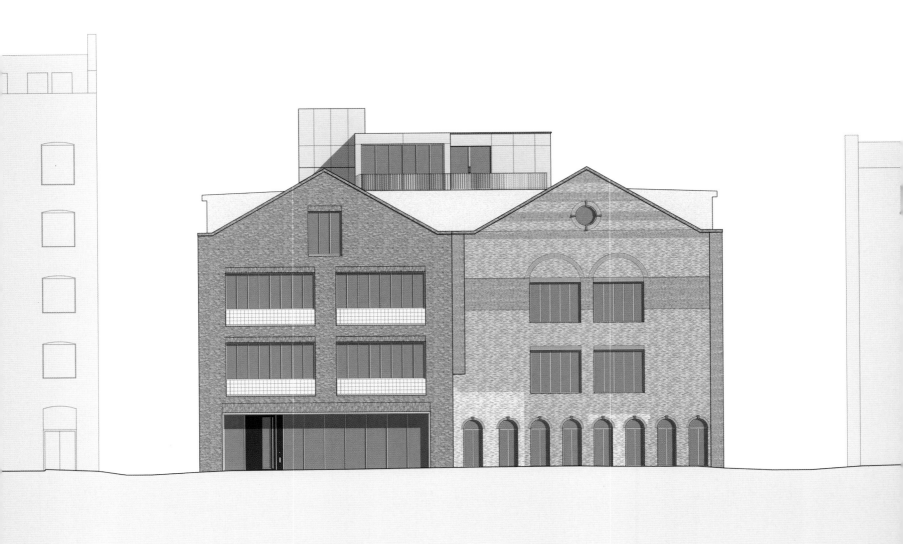

Opposite West elevation.

Right At the join of new and old, it can be seen how the new facade reflects and complements the character of the original warehouse.

Below The north–south section shows the contrast between the existing concrete-encased steel structure (left) and the more delicate new steel frame.

Opposite Upper-floor (top) and ground-floor plans.

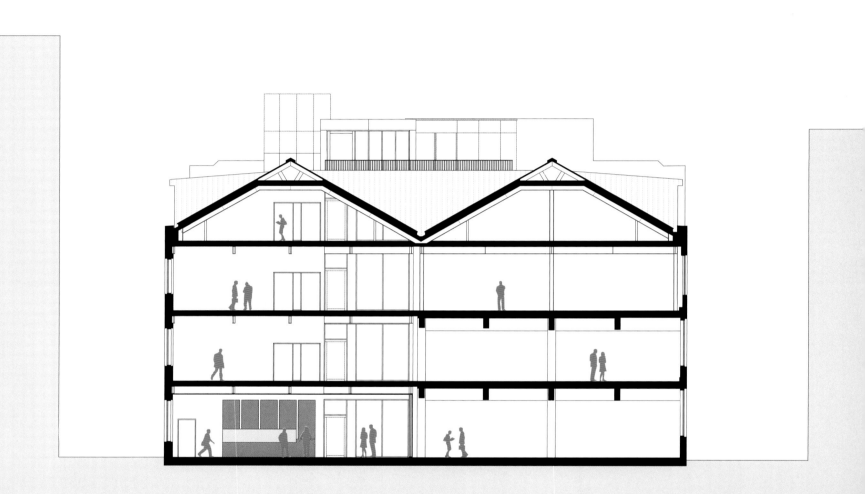

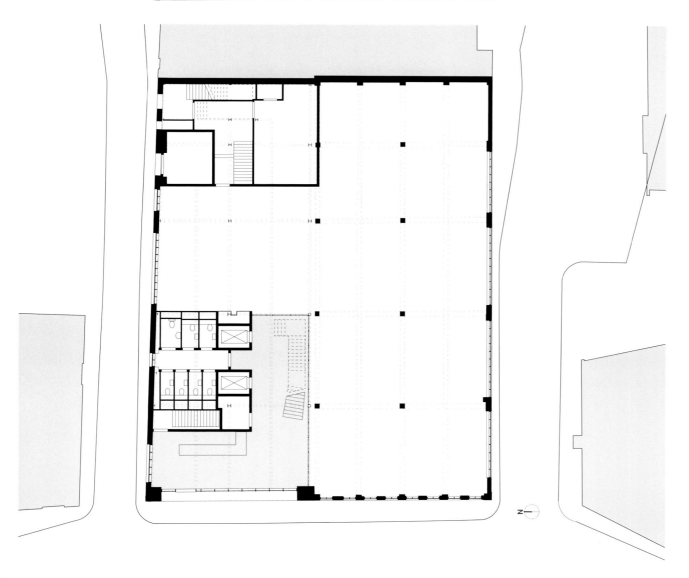

PROJECT DATA

LOCATION
Southwark, London

CLIENT
Morgan Capital Partners

SIZE
4,000 square metres

START DATE
2012

COMPLETION DATE
2017

The new building enhances the
historic character of the area and
ties into improvements that have
been made to the street and the
public realm.

The roof-level dormers create an additional floor across the whole site without appearing to increase the massing. Seen here (clockwise from top) are the roof terrace, the central staircase and the side elevation.

A guiding principle of the interior architecture was to use solid materials, such as brickwork and polished concrete.

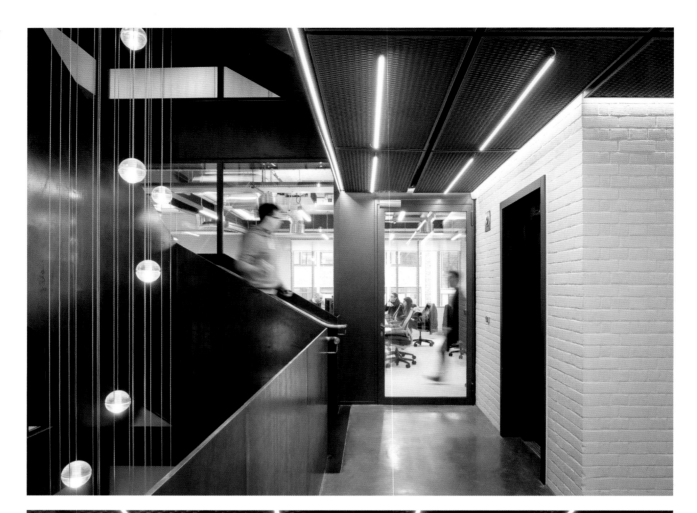

This page The impeccable finish of the central staircase is continued into the reception area.

Overleaf The staircase stitches the building together, drawing natural light down from the light well above, which is complemented by dramatic handmade hanging lights.

Katie Tonkinson

At Hawkins\Brown, we are fortunate to have been given the opportunity to design almost every sort of building. In fact, we have expanded the practice on the back of just that; we have always been 'mixed-use' architects.

Mixing uses can solve problems, increase complexity and lead to a richer design and new types of space. It can mean that a site is used more intensively and in a more viable way, and also accommodate sharing infrastructure, car parking and open spaces. For instance, by bringing workspace and flats together, we extend a site's hours of use, making it more active and safer, and offering more to the neighbourhood. We provide opportunities for people to work locally, flexibly and sustainably. In busy cities, it is often better to place a workplace, shop, school or college on a ground floor or in a basement than to use such areas for residential space.

Neighbourhood planning

When we are commissioned for a new building project – regardless of the scale or type – we like to understand it in the context of the neighbourhood and community it serves, and that often triggers a mixed-use approach, whether it is a small school, a masterplan for a large residential development or any building type or scale in between. Does that small community centre also need a cafe to generate revenue and daycare to support local families? Should this new university research facility also promote a space where local schools can be invited to share the learning? Are those thousands of new homes spread across a mix of different tenures, for residents of differing needs? Is the mixed-use masterplan a good fit for the neighbourhood, and does it mimic adjacent sites, or does it bring

something new and distinctly different to the area? Does a transport hub suggest growth, and can we start to mix scale as well as use?

Much of this thinking harks back to a simple approach to neighbourhood planning that effectively balances housing with good 'walkable' amenities such as health care, nurseries and schools, shops and pleasant open space. Each neighbourhood should be overlaid with a network of accessible transport modes, or have a transport hub at its heart, so that each mixed-use community is connected to its neighbours.

In reality, the shape, structure and size of cities, towns and neighbourhoods vary tremendously across the United Kingdom, and few experience balance and growth. To date, shifting patterns in industry have been a major factor in how mixed-use developments come about, and since the late twentieth century the trend has been for modern industry to move out towards city boundaries and inner-city mills and factories to be converted for new – usually mixed – use. This displacement of industry, alongside investment in new and extended transport infrastructure, contributes to changes in the distribution of urban populations. Population demographics have a significant bearing not only on the mix of uses, but also on the quality. In terms of living, the city centre is still often seen as the domain of the well-off and the homeless, while inner-city areas still suffer higher unemployment and must often accommodate larger migrant populations. This in turn affects the value of land and willingness to invest.

It is interesting to see how the classification of Public Transport Accessibility Levels affects the scale at which a range of mixed-use components might be introduced on a site.

A high rating reflects an accessible environment and often encourages growth and clusters of tall buildings. Tall buildings help to enliven our cities; they also help us to fit a lot of homes and other mixed-use into a relatively small amount of space. In my view, it is appropriate to promote high-density development at these key nodes, as long as all the necessary social infrastructure is in place to support those communities.

What makes architects anxious are tools such as the 'child yield calculator', which are used where a big new population is known to be incoming, to make sure that contributions are made to schooling as an essential mixed-use component of a neighbourhood. Such a mechanical method results in a condition that can be answered by payment – and, in my mind, that is simply not acceptable. It appears to take no account of the condition or capacity of existing schools, nor does it stop the funds generated from being smeared thinly across the wider school district, rather than having an impact on local families in need.

While local authorities know that bigger regeneration sites require a mix of uses, many development frameworks simply give a percentage of the whole that the authorities would like to see developed into uses other than residential. We sometimes work with property market researchers to develop the brief for mixed-use sites.

We recently used a method that had previously been used only to plan large-scale masterplans – the regeneration of Ebbsfleet in Kent, for example – to shape the brief for a smaller 5-hectare site: the Wharves, Deptford, where we had been commissioned to design a mixed-use development. I was sceptical that we could use a scientific tool to calculate something

Approaching Mixed-use

that in my mind needed working out in a more human way. But the brief that developed was very clever. It analysed the wider area, looking at the population and a range of census data. It also registered how that population might be changing by plotting proposed development in the same area. This was particularly important for the site we were looking at, since there were numerous historic industrial sites near by that had been allocated for redevelopment, and the area was being regenerated apace.

The study went on to identify a couple of thriving and 'successful' areas that it deemed to be 'similar', with catchments that threw up comparable census data, distance from transport nodes, geographical features and so on. It plotted the mix of businesses in that area using data from the Office of National Statistics and Companies House, and recorded each business establishment and other unit in respect of their Standard Industrial Classification code, so that we could begin to understand the type and scale of economic activity in the area. All this information was used to generate the baseline brief, which provided a detailed mix of commercial, retail, hospitality, leisure and community uses. It went into even more detail within each; for example, commercial was divided into warehouses, offices with storage, fronted offices, small studios and so on.

The final mixed-use brief evolved through collaboration with the estate agent Savills and discussion with the client and design team, and used this unique method, underpinned by real-life data. This resulted in a far richer set of design criteria that allowed us to begin to shape a more believable mixed-use masterplan to serve the old guard and new community alike.

Mixing commercial space

We are currently looking at a large brownfield site on the edge of the Manchester City core, with a transport node at its heart – a really exciting starting point for a new mixed-use community. Our client is committed to linking the site to its context with new, well-positioned streets and a new canal crossing. He is also committed to creating public realm with a generous new square and street-level activity. The site is being promoted for a creative campus of workspaces. This brings crucial investment into an area that in the last few years has focused on promoting the redevelopment of sites for new homes, but where money has also gone into a new health centre, a new school and new tram infrastructure.

On the face of it, the brief seems to suggest anything but a mix of uses. If a set of planning drawings existed, they would read 'B1 Commercial'. However, we have worked carefully with our client to understand who might make the vision for this site, and together we have plotted the potential development capacity across a much broader set of commercial mixed-use types, including 'Makers', 'Incubators/Start-ups', 'Co-Working', 'Technology, Media & Communications', 'Graded Office', 'Support System' and 'Cultural Warehouse'. These uses are to be provided for by taking inspiration from everything from the flatted factories of 1960s Singapore to today's 'New Lab' (a community of New York City's leading advanced-technology companies in a historic Brooklyn Navy Yard building). In this instance, mixed-use is about expanding the way we think about the commercial sector, developing a masterplan and a narrative to describe the people we want to attract, and setting out a range of workplaces that are differentiated in their architecture, amenities, servicing, setting, specification and rental cost.

Shifting economic and social conditions, and the need to think in a sustainable way about our cities, our buildings and the space between, make mixed-use something that we as architects should always have on our checklist. My own neighbourhood, Altrincham, to the southwest of Manchester, has great walkable amenities, transport and social infrastructure, and is surrounded by prosperous neighbourhoods and good schools. Yet in 2012 it came top in a 'ghost town' survey, boasting the highest percentage of boarded-up shops, after a combination of online retail and the 'Tesco effect' had a huge impact. In the last few years, with the help of significant investment from the council and from Nick Johnson and his team at Market Operations, the town centre has reinvented itself. The old market hall and neighbouring structures – both old and new – now house some of the best food vendors in a new-style space that includes a brilliant communal dining area. The success of the regenerated market has rubbed off on the rest of the town, which has in turn adjusted its DNA of mixed-use and begun to revive itself with different businesses and renewed confidence.

At Hawkins\Brown, we will continue to enjoy working with a mixed-use palette. We look forward to designing and building the best places for people's needs, for the here and now and with flexibility for change, in buildings old and new and over bigger masterplans, with reference to the past and with an eye to future generations.

The 800 pupils of the independent City of London Freemen's School (CLFS) returned for the spring term in January 2014 to a distressing sight: the building that had housed their 25-metre swimming pool was now a sorry pile of wet ash and burned remains. All that stood was a small set of showers. Just a few nights earlier, a fire had broken out and spread quickly through the structure, which was mainly of timber. Despite the efforts of eight firefighting crews, the building collapsed just three hours later.

It was a sad loss to the school, but thankfully the only loss. Fortunately, there was plenty of separation between the pool and other buildings. The school's name belies its location – not in the dense urban environment of the City of London but some 25 kilometres southwest of the Square Mile, in leafy Surrey. Founded in 1854 by the Corporation of London to educate orphans of the Freemen of the City (citizens granted valuable rights to trade), the school is now set in 23 hectares of lawns and woodland in Ashtead Park.

A new era

There was good fortune also in the fact that the pool building was far from new. In fact, it was due to be replaced as part of a ten-year programme of improvements and additions, by the end of which the school was aiming to have increased its roll by 50 per cent.

The masterplan for the expansion and reinvigoration of the school campus had been drawn up by Hawkins\Brown in 2010. A series of phased projects would include the refurbishment of Grade II*-listed Main House to create a sixth-form centre, and the demolition of a collection of 1960s buildings to make way for a new dining hall, a junior school and an assembly hall. The replacement of the swimming-pool building was originally to be carried out as part of Phase 3, but the fire made it a more pressing undertaking. Work on the new pool was brought forward, to give the pupils a functioning facility as quickly as possible.

The school was looking for a high-quality, inspirational building, in line with the rest of the development programme. Quality of facilities is crucial in the race to remain competitive within the independent schools heartland of southeast England, and to attract new pupils and families to the sector. CLFS was determined to procure excellent, modern facilities that were sympathetic to their historic and natural surroundings.

The landscape at Ashtead Park is protected with a Grade II listing, which meant that the new pool building had to be designed and located to minimize its impact on views from historic Main House. Planning consent also depended on the designers' ability to conceal the building's bulk within the landscape.

Lying low

The pool was moved from the west of the campus to woodland on the eastern side, close to the sports hall and all-weather playing fields but separate from the academic heart of the school. Hawkins\Brown's solution took advantage of a fall across the site to nestle the building into the landscape. The storerooms and changing rooms, none of which required windows, were partially submerged in a lower ground floor, which helped the building to lie lower in the landscape, reducing its visual impact. A reception and teaching room were placed alongside the double-height pool hall, while the considerable volume of mechanical and electrical equipment needed for the pool has been concealed, leaving glazing along three sides of the building.

Above the bathers would stand a structure with its own natural elegance. A series of white-stained timber arches, each with its apex at a different point, creates a roof ridge that follows the main axis of movement: from the entrance in one corner, through to the pool hall and diagonally across the rectangular pool to the opposite corner. The shifting form of the frames creates the sense of a wave rippling through the hall, above the heads of the swimmers.

Opposite On a quiet day the simplicity of the pool hall's design provides a peaceful, relaxing space with views out to the surrounding woodland.

Right The new building nestles into the landscape, and trees help to shield the building when seen from the main house.

City of London Freemen's School Swimming Pool

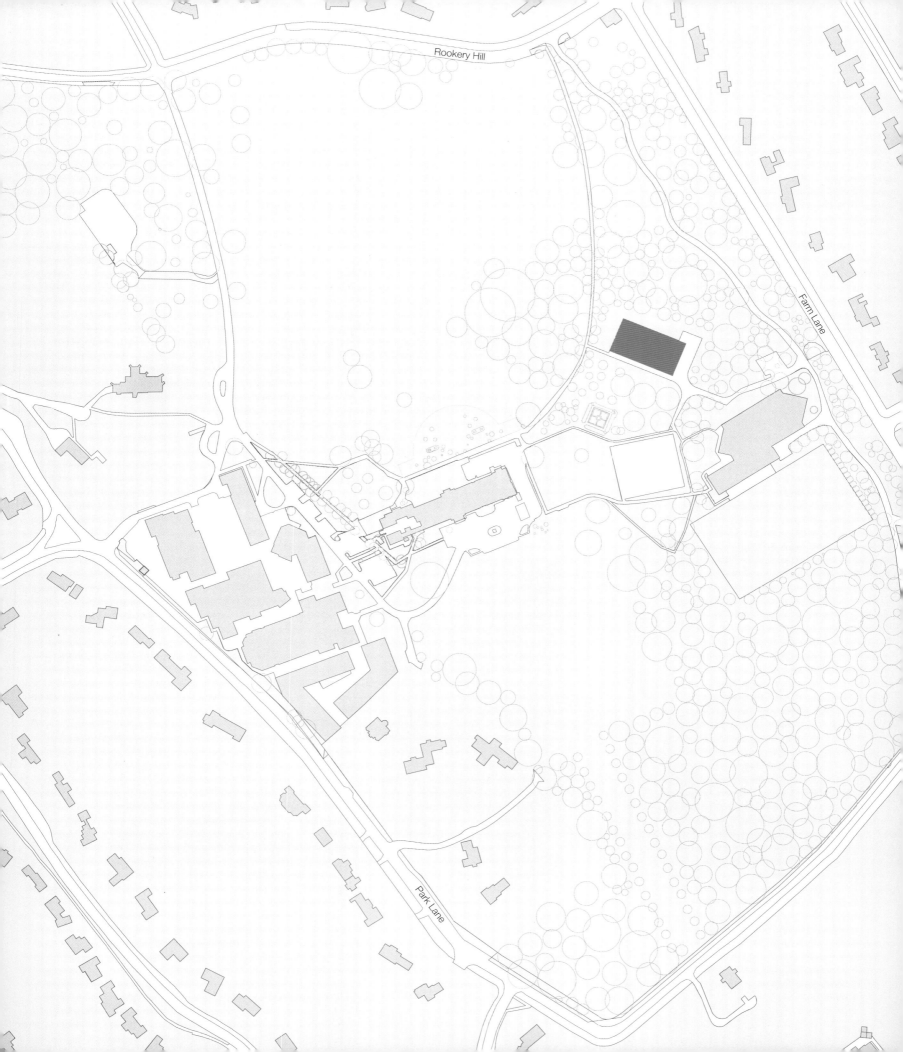

Rookery Hill

Farm Lane

Park Lane

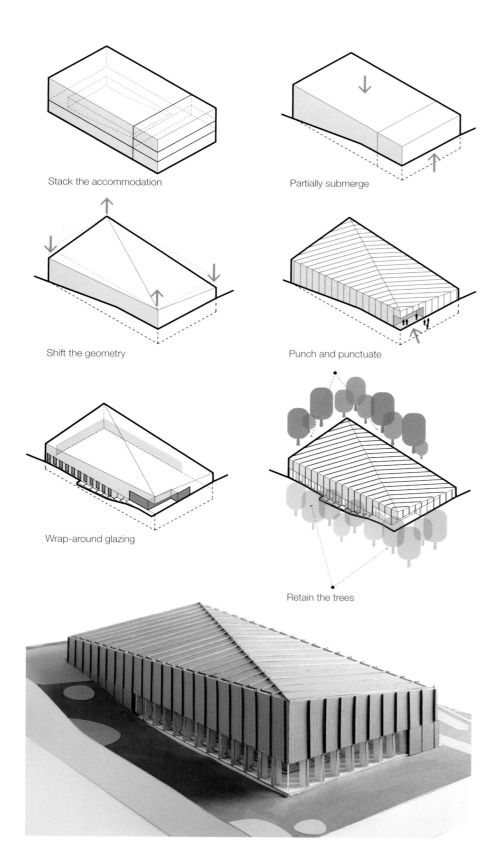

Stack the accommodation

Partially submerge

Shift the geometry

Punch and punctuate

Wrap-around glazing

Retain the trees

A model created to explore
the building's form, materiality
and detailing.

Natural advantages

The all-timber structure was fabricated off-site from two different kinds of engineered wood: glued laminated timber (glulam) for the arches, and bracing wall and roof panels of cross-laminated timber (CLT). Glulam's layering of timber sections allows the fabrication of large, sophisticated, high-strength structural shapes that would be impossible with solid-sawn timber. CLT's alternating layers of timber placed crosswise to one another increase its strength and rigidity. The white staining of both allowed the timber structure to meet statutory spread-of-flame requirements.

Timber offers clear advantages over steel and concrete for pool buildings. It is a natural insulator, so the structure itself contributes to the building's thermal envelope. This also significantly reduces the risk of condensation forming on the exposed internal structure. Hawkins\Brown were keen to prevent the dripping of condensation on to spectators and swimmers, a problem that occurs in some steel-framed pool halls. A timber frame is also much less costly to maintain. A pool hall is a corrosive environment for steel, and the structure must be repainted every year or two to keep it protected.

The other advantage of timber for CLFS was its speed of construction. The school needed a replacement pool in double-quick time to prevent current pupils from losing out and to reassure those thinking of joining the school. The relative complexity of the structure could have posed a challenge, but the architect was able to share the 3D model with the timber contractor, who used it as the basis for milling the beams and connection points. Once on site, the entire timber structure – the glulam portal frame and the CLT walls and roof – was erected in just over three weeks. This allowed the detailed design and full construction of the building to be carried out in a year.

Outside, the new pool hall responds to its setting. A traditional, hand-formed standing-seam cladding, dark copper in colour, wraps the building above the glazing, echoing key features of Main House and integrating the structure into the surrounding woodland. In the entrance area, a rhythm of red cedar battens references the materials of the new music school, which was completed as part of Phase 1. The pupils of CLFS are now able to sample swimming among the trees, since the wraparound glazing and deep but slender timber columns allow clear views from the water into the woodland of Ashtead Park beyond.

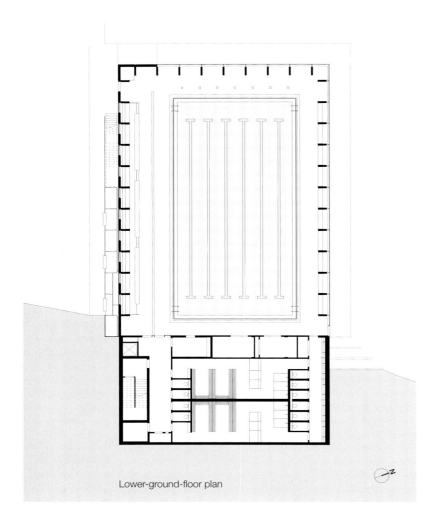

Lower-ground-floor plan

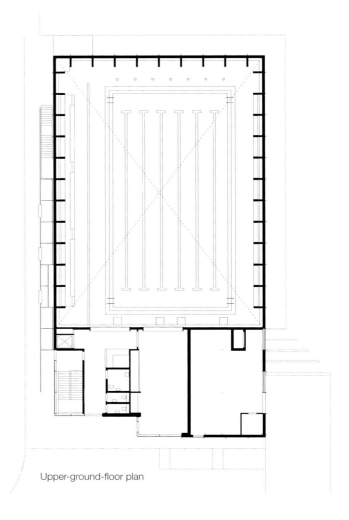

Upper-ground-floor plan

East–west section.

PROJECT DATA

LOCATION
Ashtead, Surrey, UK

CLIENT
City of London Freemen's School

SIZE
1,750 square metres

START DATE
2014

COMPLETION DATE
2015

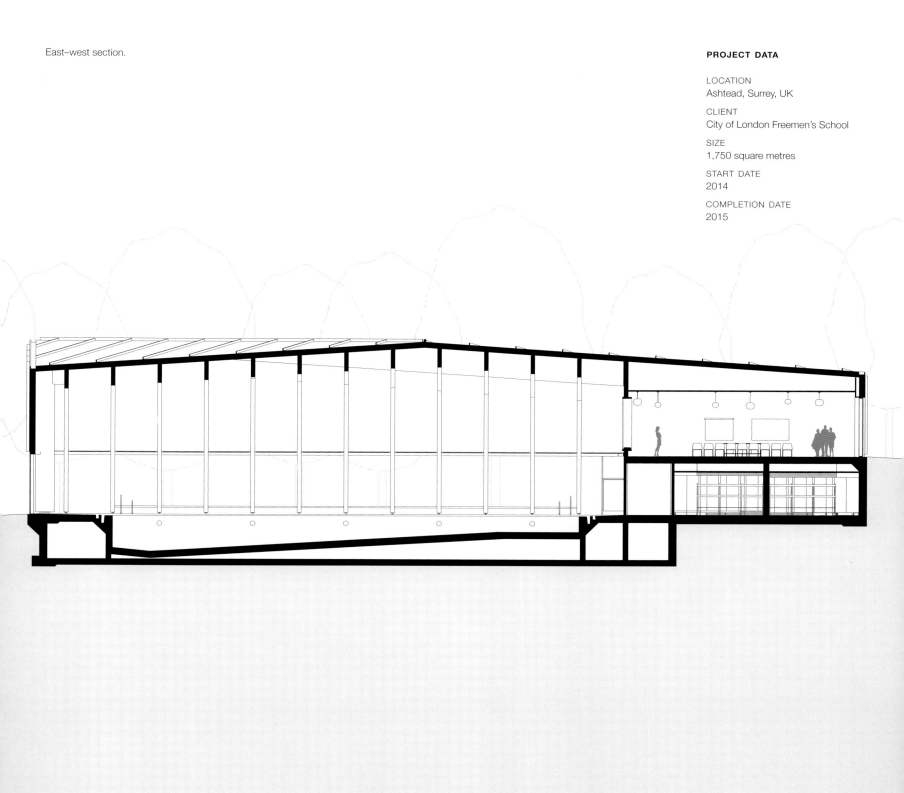

The building was relocated to consolidate the school's sports facilities and offer the wider community an easily accessible pool in a beautiful setting.

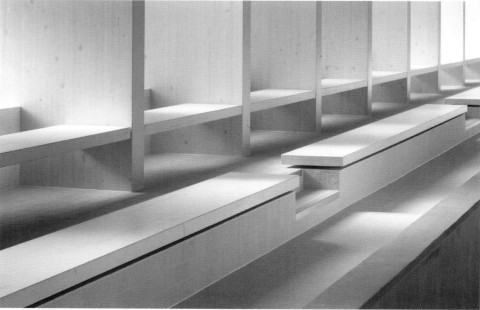

Deep window seats line the pool hall, reception and event space, engaging visitors with the woodland surroundings as well as with the activity in the pool.

As part of the project, the surrounding landscape was planted with native woodland species including more than thirty new trees and hundreds of understorey plants.

Right The form of the building takes shape as the timber frame is constructed.

Below Hand-formed dark copper standing-seam cladding responds to the historic features of the school's main house and help to meld building and landscape.

Overleaf The new building provides a robust backdrop to the social splash and buzz of a swimming session.

The University of Oxford is the oldest university in the English-speaking world, and teaching is thought to have started there in the eleventh century. In that context, Hawkins\Brown's ten-year residency as one of the university's preferred architects represents a drop in a temporal ocean. But the relationship with the university has outlasted those of many other architects. More importantly, the projects that have come out of this partnership are having a significant impact on the quality of architecture and research at one of the world's most eminent seats of learning.

Designing for Oxford University means meeting the exceptional standards and demands of highly discriminating users from all over the world. It means earning the trust of Oxford City Council planners and the university's academics, estates department, donors and other stakeholders. This requires inventive, well-researched, uncompromising designs that meet their different demands. And it means creating sophisticated, high-performance buildings that can balance relevance to modern architecture with reverence for their august surroundings.

Crucial to the relationship with the university has been the mix of skills within Hawkins\Brown, which has allowed the practice to adapt to the university's wide-ranging needs. From single-floor refurbishments to new landmark buildings, and from a GP's surgery to a vibration-free basement for the study of sub-atomic particles, the range in scale and function of the different projects could not be wider.

The Biochemistry building: Rethinking the Science Area

The creation of a new home for the Department of Biochemistry laid the groundwork for the relationship. This internationally celebrated building changed the DNA of the largest biochemistry department in the UK, introducing more dynamic, collaborative working by turning the conventional design of university research buildings inside out. Instead of occupying the core of the building, laboratories were arranged on the perimeter of each floor, creating a central, daylit atrium where scientists could easily have chance encounters, strike up conversations and sow the seeds of new partnerships. The labs become the shop window for the department and for science generally. At night, a strata-like colour scheme along the science corridors combines with the coloured glass

fins running up and down the facade, transforming the building into an eye-catching, polychromatic stage for high-level scientific activity.

In the year following the building's opening, applications to study biochemistry at Oxford rose by 50 per cent, and in its annual trawl of outstanding postgraduates, every one of the department's top five choices accepted the offer of a research position in the building. Discussion, interaction and collaboration are taking place on a whole new level between academics with different scientific interests, generating more scientific papers, more research projects and grants, and more discoveries. The second phase of the Biochemistry building is now at an advanced stage of design.

A physical departure
Further advanced, but still under construction at the time of writing, the new Department of Physics builds

Opposite A detail of the Beecroft Building's copper-alloy facade.

Right Hawkins\Brown's highly acclaimed Biochemistry building was the first major project in the transformation of the university's Science Area. Phase 1 was completed in 2008 and phase 2 is set to be completed in 2020.

University of Oxford
Beecroft Building

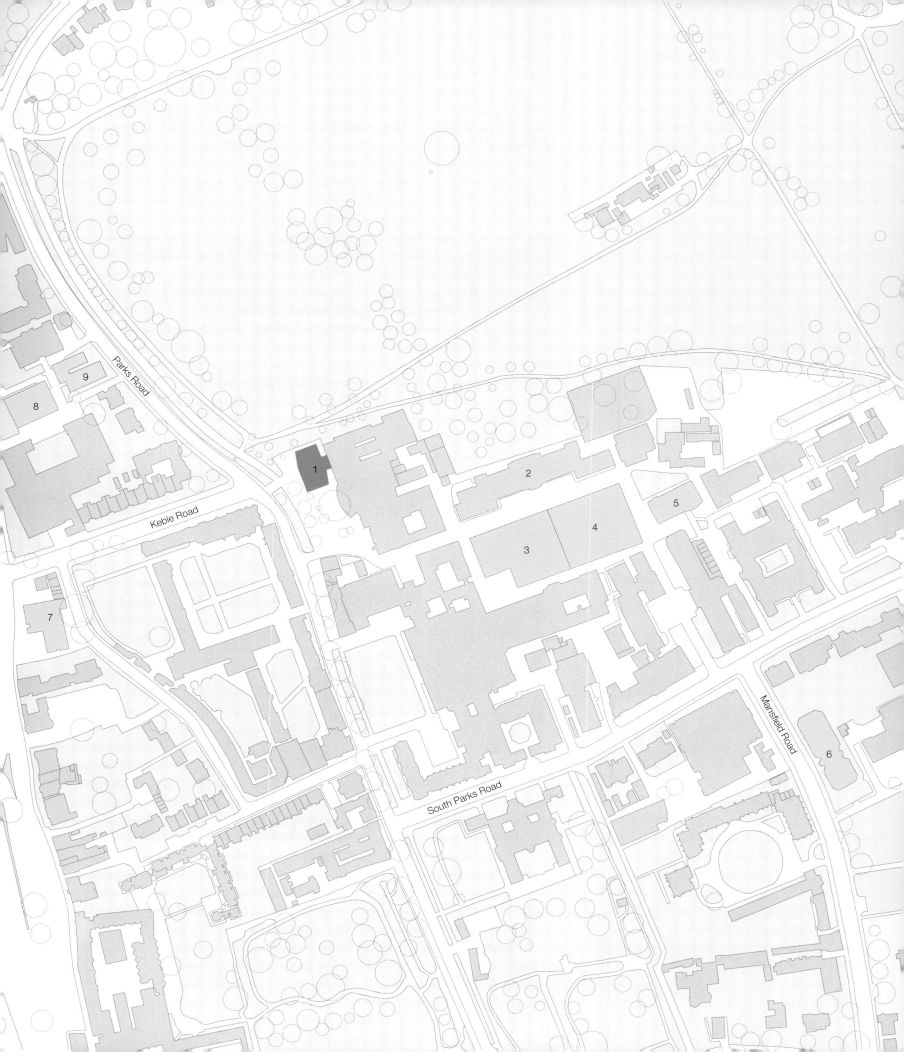

Parks Road

9

8

1

Keble Road

2

5

3

4

7

Mansfield Road

6

South Parks Road

A model shows the Beecroft Building in context.

on the achievements of the Biochemistry building. It, too, assembles in a single workplace scientists who previously mixed only with others from their own specialist fields, in smaller, older, outdated premises. And it takes the inside-out thinking of Biochemistry as the basis for its design, adapting it for working practices from a different science.

The Beecroft Building (as it will be known) will be a very different creature from Biochemistry, though. It brings together two separate research disciplines, Theoretical Physics and Experimental Physics, in a structure that is divided into two very distinct halves. Above ground will be soundproofed offices and informal, collaborative 'platforms'. Below ground, a five-storey basement will house vibration-free, 'black box' labs – some of the most advanced in the world – where scientists will work at the very edge of what is possible in a laboratory.

Providing the final piece in the jigsaw of the Physics Department complex, in the northwest corner of the university's Science Area, the building occupies one of Oxford's most sensitive sites. The 200 scientists who will use it have previously been scattered across the university estate, occasionally gathering around blackboards to hear and discuss new lines of thought. The antiquated warrens

of offices, isolated from one another, have limited the potential for team thinking and collaboration, and deterred leading physicists from making a move to Oxford.

Interaction and solitude

In a briefing day held on the site for the five shortlisted architecture practices who took part in the original competition, Professor John Wheater, Oxford's Head of Physics, outlined his vision for a working environment that combined interaction and solitude. With the aid of chalk diagrams on his own blackboard, Wheater proposed a completely open and transparent environment that would allow scientists to come together and share ideas in a common space, but also to work in their own individual rooms in total silence.

Such an environment would ideally occupy a low, flat building, with offices and studies arranged around a large, spacious collaboration area. On this site, however, with protected structures and public space on all sides, that was never going to be possible. The compact brownfield plot lies across Parks Road from Sir William Butterfield's Grade I-listed Victorian Gothic chapel (1876) at Keble College, with University Parks, also listed, immediately

One of the specialized experimental laboratory spaces for Cryogenics nears completion.

to the north. Other buildings – protected by a conservation area – hem the site in to the west and south.

The new accommodation would have to be stacked vertically, over a number of levels, rather than horizontally. Hawkins\Brown's solution keeps the acoustically separate individual and group offices on the perimeter of the building, spread over five storeys. The group working areas – each orientated around a blackboard – are positioned within the central atrium, but on linked platforms at half-floor levels. This allows the action taking place on each platform to be observed from offices and landings above and below, and breaks the large central space into smaller, more intimate zones that invite interaction and teamwork.

The design team developed the detail of the group thinking space with the intense involvement of the Physics Department's research team, to create an environment

that is as encouraging as possible to collaboration. Their intention was to create a hive of activity buzzing with debate that can draw scientists throughout the building into the lively discussions going on around them.

Experimental Physics requires a very different kind of accommodation. A further five storeys below ground will hold state-of-the-art laboratories for world-class research in the fields of nanotechnology, quantum properties of materials, quantum optics and atomic force microscopy. The sophisticated technology and heavy, high-precision machinery necessary for studying the activity of atomic particles demand a tightly controlled environment that is completely free of vibration.

A lower suite of experimental laboratories, including 'black box' labs, requires an entire floor of damping equipment below it to isolate it from subterranean vibrations as well as from the vibration generated within the building. Above the lab floor sits a level of air-conditioning and other services, followed by another lab floor and a further storey of services.

The passage of the building through planning was challenging. Apart from the fact that it is a major construction project – including the excavation and piling of a 16-metre-deep basement – very close to listed structures, the Beecroft Building promises to alter the entire dynamic of this gateway to the city centre, potentially presenting a visual counterpoint to Keble chapel, across Parks Road.

Hawkins\Brown carefully developed the massing and facade design in response to the surrounding spaces and buildings, influenced not only by Keble but also by more contemporary Oxford buildings, such as St Catherine's College, designed in the 1960s by Arne Jacobsen. The resulting vertical rhythm around the building's facade has been established with weathered copper-alloy fins, stepped in height and depth to break down the five-storey mass. Double-height picture windows in the collaboration areas offer important views in and out.

The contextual approach won over Oxford City Council, a process that was aided by the good relationship developed between the architects and planning authority in the creation of the Biochemistry building. Councillors praised the design's use of the available space, its low environmental impact and its low carbon footprint. Despite the heavy servicing of the Experimental Physics labs, the building was able to achieve an Excellent BREEAM rating.

The iceberg-style arrangement of space – half above ground, half below – has made special demands on the construction. Hawkins\Brown has continued its collaboration from the Biochemistry building with the contractor Laing O'Rourke, adopting cutting-edge construction techniques and a great deal of prefabrication. The floors of the subterranean Experimental Physics labs include 'keel slabs': 2.5-metre-deep concrete blocks – the heaviest of which weigh 54 tonnes – mounted on damping systems that provide the perfect platform for nano-scale experiments, isolated from the tiniest vibration in the rest of the structure. To minimize the transmission of vibration, noise, dust and inconvenience to Beecroft's venerable neighbours, including the chapel of Keble College, the pre-cast concrete frame and cladding system were fabricated and assembled off-site, and transported to Oxford in modules for rapid construction.

A new powerhouse of physics research

The University of Oxford will soon have a world-class building to match the global reputation of its physics research. Above ground, the central thinking spaces will buzz with discussion and ideas; all around, scientists will be able to watch equations and theories grow on blackboards, even from behind the soundproof glass screens of their offices. In the numerous meeting areas and walkways, theoretical physicists will be able to mingle with experimental physicists, whose study will be concentrated in the UK's most advanced physics laboratories, below ground. In helping to attract the finest staff and students from around the world, and place them together in a setting made for collective thinking, the Beecroft Building will transform the practice of physics at Oxford.

Below All services are suspended using anti-vibration springs.

Below, right One of the eighteen vibration-mitigating keel slabs *in situ*. These slabs provide a stable surface for laboratory experiments above.

PROJECT DATA

LOCATION
Oxford, UK

CLIENT
University of Oxford Estates
Directorate and Department
of Physics

SIZE
5,500 square metres

START DATE
2011

COMPLETION DATE
2018

Below The floor plans are highlighted to show the link from the existing Clarendon Laboratory building into the central atrium and mezzanines.

Opposite Section showing the organization of the building. Theoretical Physics occupies the upper levels, while Experimental laboratories make use of the stable conditions below ground.

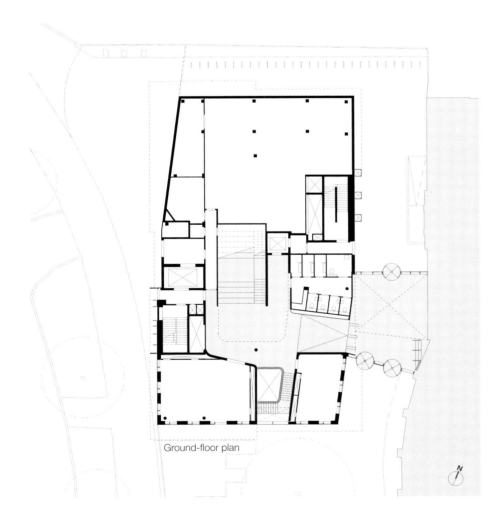

Ground-floor plan

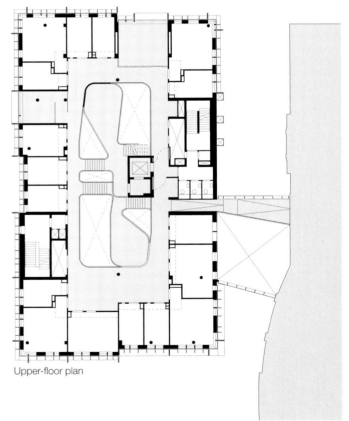

Upper-floor plan

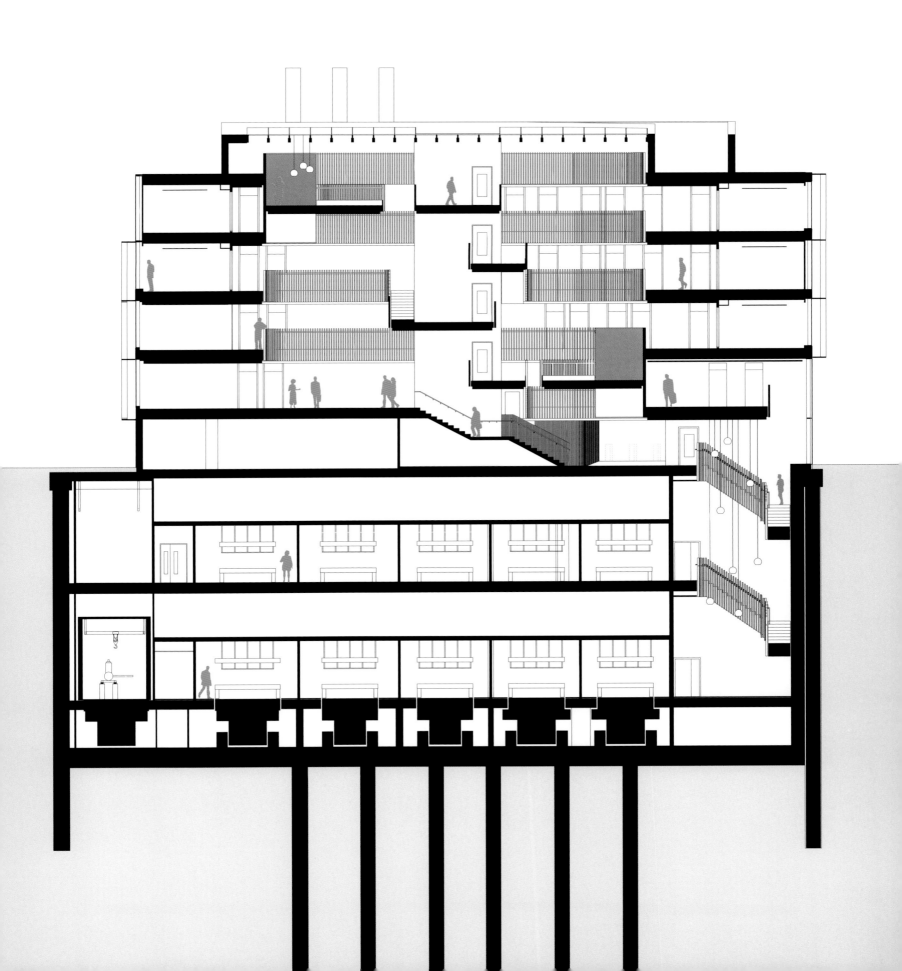

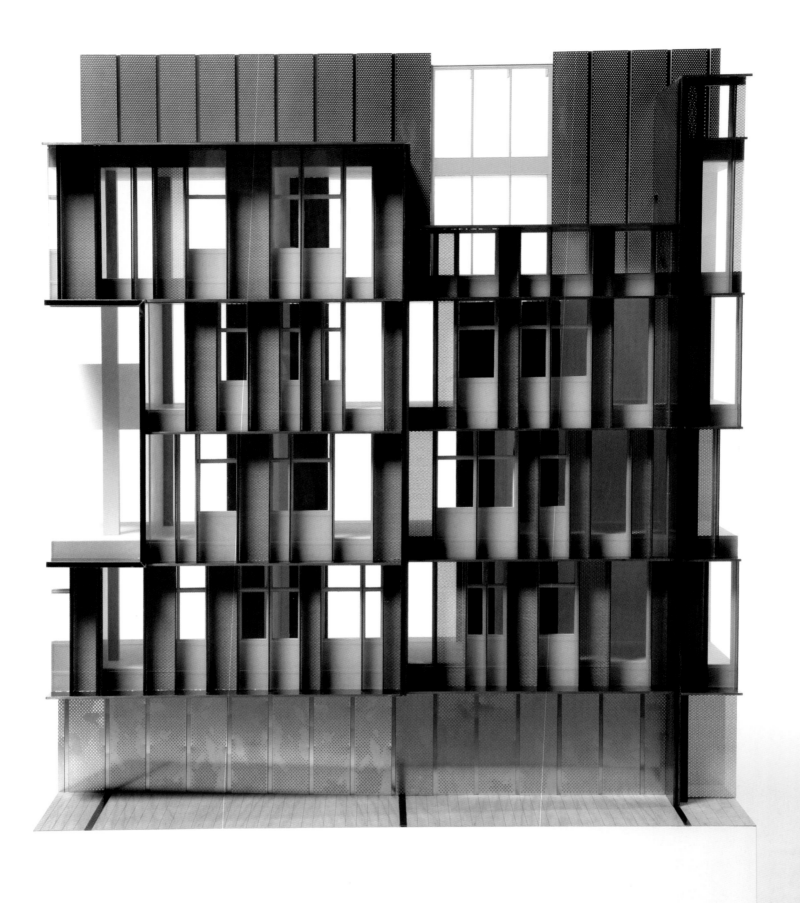

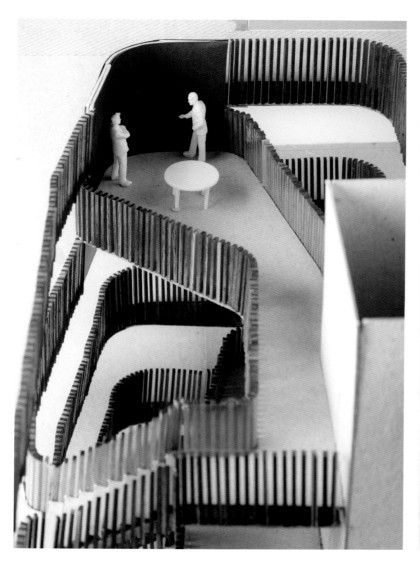

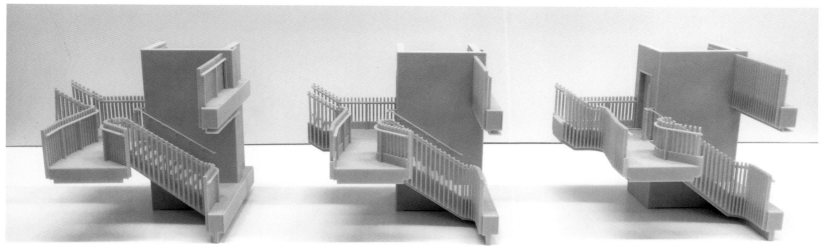

Opposite A detailed study model of the facade materials.

Top Handmade study models of the atrium were created to help users understand the collaborative platforms in three dimensions.

Above 3D-printed study models of the atrium stair were used during the design process to test construction details.

The double-height curved blackboards central to the organization of the building take shape during construction (right), and are envisaged as a social, collaborative tool during the design process (below).

A cross-section visualization depicts the two halves of the building linked by the central stairs and atrium.

Excavation on site illustrates the scale of the 16-metre-deep basement and its proximity to the listed buildings beyond.

Details from the internal fit-out and installation of the fin balustrade and collaboration platforms in the atrium.

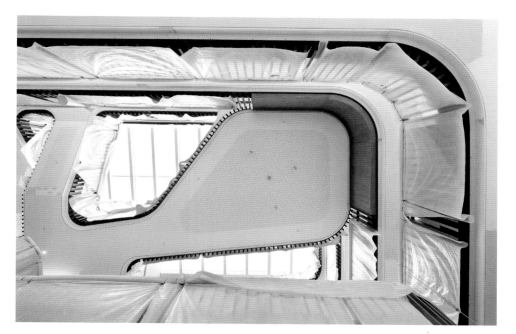

The materials of the facade
respond to and complement
the neighbouring Grade I-listed
chapel of Keble College by
Sir William Butterfield.

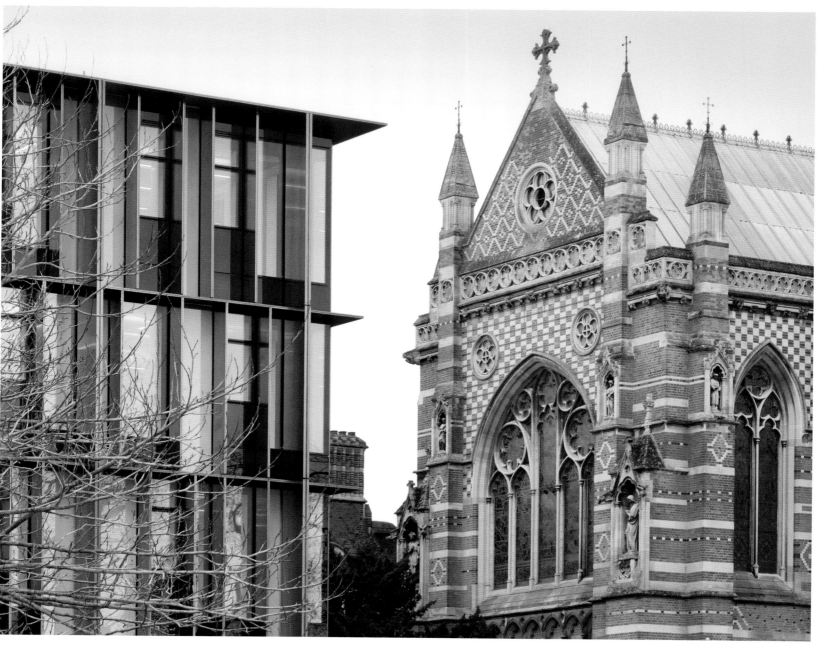

Harbinder Singh Birdi

On a recent visit to Egypt, I discussed with lecturers and students from the Cairo School of Architecture the challenges that lay ahead for the country, and what they as architects could do to meet them. We debated the political upheaval, unrest and instability and the effect it has had on tourism – the lifeblood of the country; and we talked about mass migration to the major cities and the pressure it has placed on existing infrastructure. We spoke about the resources, energy, water and food needed to sustain an ever-increasing population. These concerns have been echoed in conversations I have had in schools of architecture around the world. How should we prepare the architects of the future to deal with these challenges?

It is important to define the true attributes and skills of an architect, other than the diligent design and construction of a building within the boundary of a site. We must also think about the questions we should be asking to enable us to improve the environments in which we live. Arguably, there has never been a more challenging time to practise architecture. The population of the planet has more than doubled since the 1960s, and with mass urbanization around the world comes the need for good housing, the associated costly infrastructure and public amenities. Much is being asked of our political leaders, but the question is who now ultimately determines the way our cities are to be shaped to serve our communities.

To understand how the built form of the city must adapt in response to the constantly changing ways in which we live, work and play, architects have always found it necessary to exist within the political ecosystem in some way. By doing so we engage with a myriad of stakeholders, from local authorities, businesses, political lobbyists, and heritage and community groups to – most importantly – residents.

At Hawkins\Brown the requirement for this engagement with stakeholders is typified in our work on eight new public-realm projects along the Thames Estuary as part of the new Tideway tunnel (see pages 189–201). Our challenge is not only to design places that respond to their immediate historic and cultural context, but also to predict how these new public spaces – in arguably the most diverse city in the world – will benefit the people who will use them every day. To do this we are listening to and learning from a broad range of people and engaging with commercial and political concerns, heritage, local history and the needs of residents.

Some architects concentrate exclusively on their skill at understanding both the commercial and political environments that shape our cities, and now work as part of planning teams, instrumental in shaping government policy. Others are asked to contribute by sitting on local-authority design-review panels, challenging and informing the building designs brought forward by developers. As planning authorities struggle to keep pace with applications for development, architects often play a pivotal role in judging the work of their peers to ensure the production of good buildings of all kinds that respond creatively to the aspirations of the city.

Very rarely are architects given a fixed brief. Rather, most briefs derive from our ability to listen to, adjudicate and then communicate the wants and needs of many. Architects often challenge the norms of planning policy, debating how economically sustainable communities can be both created and maintained.

While this level of engagement is certainly nothing new for the architectural profession, it has never before been so important for us to understand policy and its impact on commerce. Since the financial crash of 2007, both in the United Kingdom and internationally, the public sector has looked more than ever to the private sector for investment to shape and regenerate cities. Governments and councils must now negotiate their assets and collaborate with private developers to share the responsibility of providing the housing and infrastructure our cities require. Central government in England, for example, now asks the newly appointed metropolitan mayors to come up with housing and infrastructure strategies to ensure the sustainable growth of their cities. In our work for London and Manchester's transport bodies, we are being asked to look for development opportunities in partnership with the private sector around each city's rail assets, to help the mayors deal with housing shortages while funding upgrades to rail infrastructure. This is no mean feat when you consider that, at the time of writing, London alone has more than 270 railway and Underground stations.

As more and more public land is handed over to the private sector to develop and maintain, an evolving role for the architect is to negotiate the existing ownership borders. On the one hand there is a requirement for an explicit border between private and public to make clear ownership and responsibilities, but on the other, it is our responsibility to ensure that all space offered up as public realm genuinely feels public, no matter who owns it.

Whether a project is public, private or multi-headed, it is of course essential for us

Shaping our Cities

It is the architect's job to untangle the chaos of the city, as beautifully depicted here by Eduardo Paolozzi in his screenprint *From Early Italian Poets*, 1974–76.

to collaborate with our clients and their team to ensure that their building succeeds in every aspect: as a commercial venture; as a representation of a brand; and as a place for people to live, learn, work and play in. No longer is the business plan hidden away; we are now expected to inform it, using our understanding of the viability and full life cycle of the buildings and spaces we design and construct.

We do this by carefully observing those who use our buildings and cities. We are noticing how education and working patterns are changing with internet connectivity and modern computing; people are no longer expected to dedicate their working time to a single place, for example. We are watching city mayors and leaders seek new ways to rid our streets of the car, fundamentally changing our transport infrastructure and public realm. We see how people choose to spend their leisure time and how global changes in retail affect our high streets and city centres.

The position of the architect was traditionally lead consultant and designer, but on most major urban projects nowadays we act as subconsultant to contractors and engineers. Because of the urgent need to regenerate and repurpose large swathes of our cities, it is becoming common for clients to rely on an emerging brand of large, commercially driven multidisciplinary organizations that promise to address any challenge the city has to offer. Working within these teams, what role do we now play and what voice does the architect have?

Some commentators believe the role of the architect is diminishing and that we have lost our ground, but it is hard to know to whom we have lost it. There is no doubt that the construction

of buildings has become more complex, and in a world where clients are advised to appoint a myriad of specialist consultants, the place of the architect must now be justified. I would argue that there is a place, however. We have learned to listen, watch and collaborate to make sense

of these complex spatial negotiations of tenure, and to integrate schools, homes and places for work and play. It would be a brave client who entrusted the responsibility to produce a well-conceived and integrated piece of architecture to anyone who was not an architect.

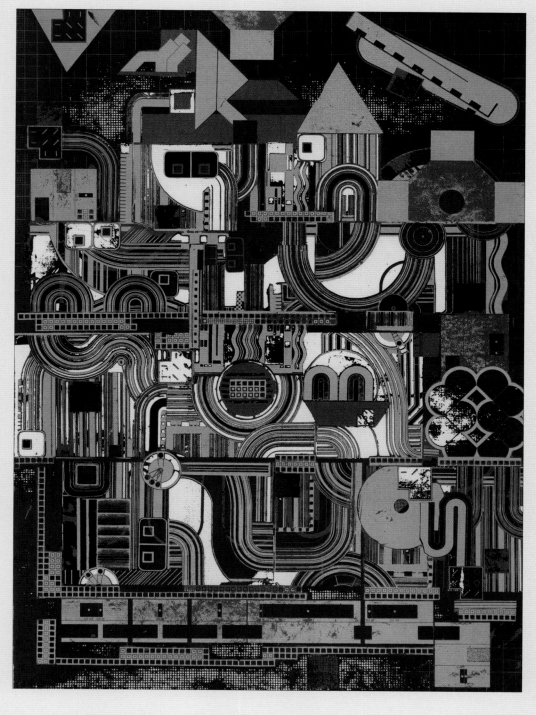

A vision of communal living, hotel-style facilities and connected, colourful architecture animates this 'build-to-rent' development next to the Queen Elizabeth Olympic Park at Stratford in east London, where an entirely new urban district is rising. As promised in London's bid for the 2012 Olympic Games, a legacy regeneration phase has transformed the area to the east of the Olympic Park. East Village, as the district is known, enjoys excellent transport connections through the rail, Tube and bus links of nearby Stratford International station, and the shopping and dining powerhouse of Westfield Stratford City is also on its doorstep.

This retail and transport infrastructure, put in place before and since 2012, has made higher-density homebuilding possible. The repurposing of the former athletes' village as affordable homes has been balanced by new tower developments offering market-rental flats in attractive, high-quality managed schemes designed to appeal to the now very wide demographic that is unable to afford the deposit on a home in a traditional London suburb.

Towards the west of the district, overlooking the wetlands of the park, East Village Plot N06 was to be a major development, offering more than 400 new homes for rent. An outline masterplan established the broad blueprint of two towers, whose height and square plan were fixed, alongside two smaller 'pavilion' blocks. The developer, Qatari Diar Delancey (QDD, a joint venture), and the landlord, Get Living London (GLL) – the partnership responsible for the build-to-rent schemes at East Village – were seeking a strategy for the 'software' or social programming of the buildings, and ideas on how the 'hardware' – the architecture – could bring a bland outline to life.

Making connections

In May 2016 a pitch meeting with Hawkins\Brown provided the direction and vitality QDD and GLL were looking for. The architects presented sketches for buildings that proposed a new level of social amenity and interaction, bringing residents together in facilities and spaces that included roof gardens, pop-up outdoor bars, a yoga studio, screening rooms, ground-floor co-working spaces and restaurants. Expanding on the emerging vision for build-to-rent of more communal living, the proposals hit the right note for the landlord. In build-to-rent, a strong social offer creates a virtuous circle of 'stickiness': well-managed social infrastructure encourages tenants to make friends, and tenants with friends around them are more likely to renew their contracts, as well as to act as brand ambassadors to their wider social group.

Architecture would set that circle in motion. The discussion at the pitch meeting led to the client and design team pulling the architectural model apart and reassembling it to maximize the connection between the buildings and reduce the cost of construction. What emerged was the concept of unifying the entire development of four buildings into a single, connected 'organism', a pair of what were being called 'towers with tails'. The design links the towers on the tenth floor via an inhabited skybridge, and then links this level, which contains many of the shared facilities, to communal gardens on the roofs of the two 'tail' blocks. The skybridge level is the beating heart of the building, and every flat is connected to it via a single internal lift journey. Corridors, lift lobbies and stairways are designed more actively as places in which to meet and dwell, and a single 'superlobby' serves the entire development.

Without the need to replicate amenities in the different blocks, more space could be given over to flats. In addition, slim-floor construction allowed the number of floors in the two towers to be raised to twenty-six and thirty-one respectively. Overall, the apartment count increased from 422 to 524 – by almost 25 per cent.

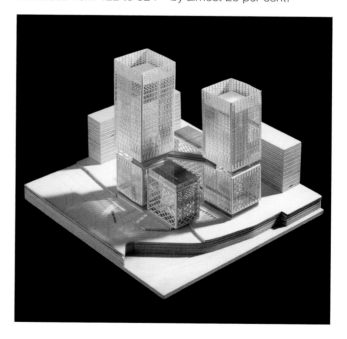

Opposite Visualization of the new development seen from the Queen Elizabeth Olympic Park.

Right A conceptual massing model highlights the communal skybridge and shared amenity spaces.

East Village Plot N06

Honour Avenue

Olympic Park Avenue

Celebration Avenue

Anthems Way

Waterden Road

Right An illustration shows how the residential, commercial and social spaces are layered.

Below An early conceptual sketch from Seth Rutt's notebook shows the 'beating heart' of the development.

A colourful contrast

With a firm vision established for the 'software', the target market for the development could be defined. QDD and GLL identified a combined demographic of 'style-seeker professionals', 'comfortable couples' and 'cool parents', who would be attracted by the mix of apartments from studio flats to three-bedroom family homes.

The design strategy for the exterior of the scheme is an expression of, and an appeal to, the sensibilities of this youngish audience. An inventive, playful application of colour across the facades animates both towers and creates a contrast with the more neutral tones of earlier East Village developments. Each tower is assigned its own palette to ground it in the wider context of the Olympic Park: five greens for the building closest to the wetlands; five reds for the southerly tower, picking up on the more vibrant dominant shades of Stratford International and Westfield. A shared secondary palette of two highlight colours, orange and blue, and two neutral colours provides a level of commonality between the buildings.

The concrete frames of the facades provide the armature for the colour. Conveying the varied hues are thousands of infill panels of bonded laminated glass, arranged horizontally and vertically to create the effect of 'clouds' of colour moving around the surface of the building, and breaking up the potentially overpowering mass of each facade. As the weather changes and daylight comes and goes, the colours shift and the character of each facade alters. Where they are transparent, such as on some balconies, the coloured panels are transformed at night in a welcoming, domestic way. As darkness falls, the facade recedes into shadow and the lobby area and tenth-floor amenity spaces emerge, lit up by a strong use of internal colour.

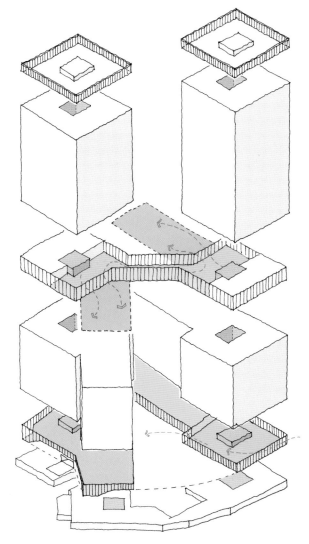

Inside the flats, residents have a choice of approach depending on their taste and budget, ranging from neutral – in which they have the freedom to add their own personality – to a fully designed set of rooms. Hawkins\Brown's interior designers worked with GLL on every element of the flats and amenity areas to ensure durability, value for money and ease of maintenance.

Learning from the hospitality sector, this scheme offers a living experience that is close to the standard of a luxury hotel. The connected design brings four sets of residents into a single community, sharing social spaces, facilities and opportunities to meet. Time and the rate of contract renewals will tell, but East Village's latest buildings may have set a new benchmark for rented living in the United Kingdom.

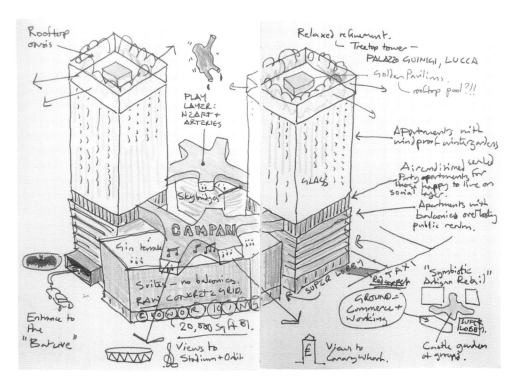

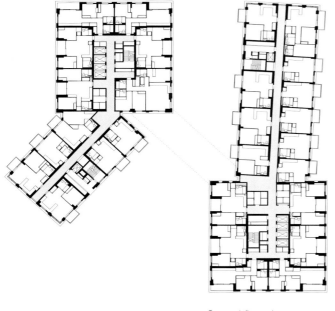

Second-floor plan

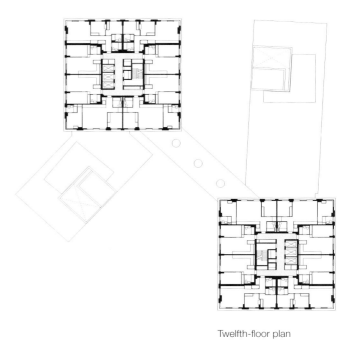

Twelfth-floor plan

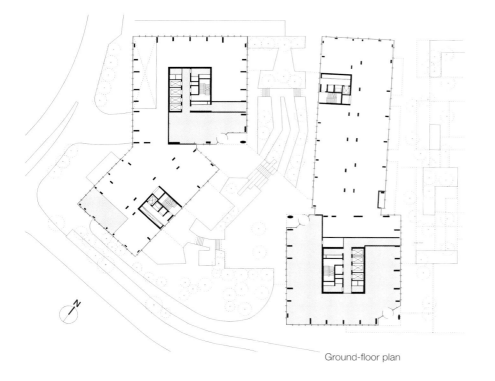

Ground-floor plan

Tenth-floor plan

Opposite West–east section.

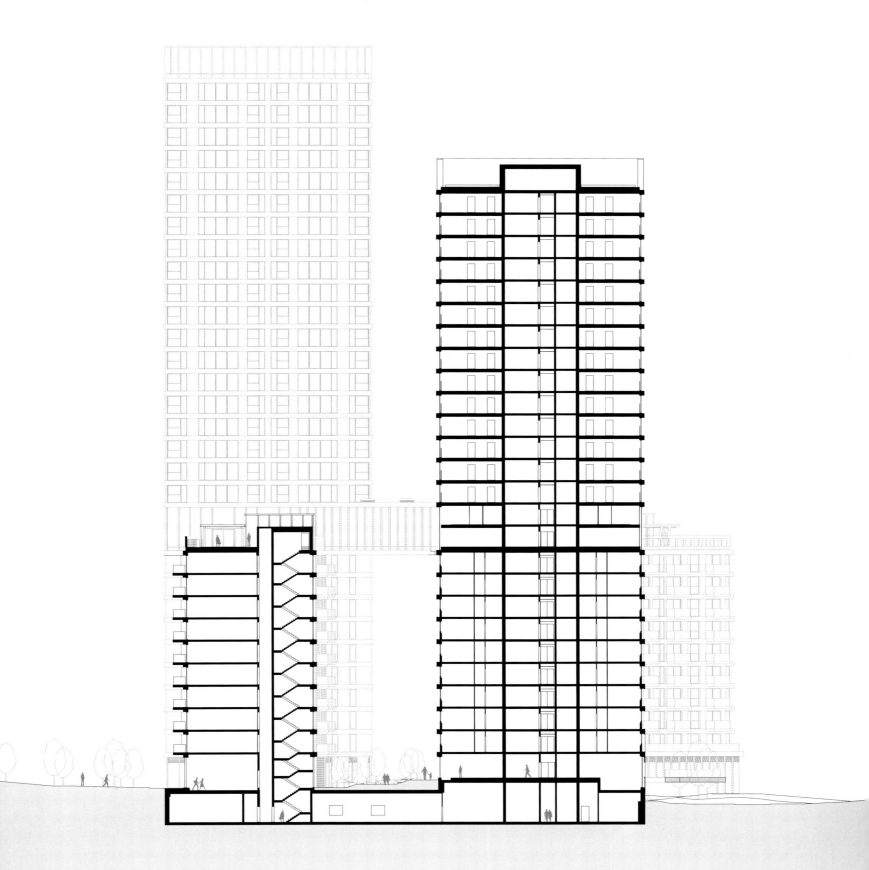

PROJECT DATA

LOCATION
Stratford, London

CLIENT
Qatari Diar; Delancey

SIZE
52,000 square metres

START DATE
2016

COMPLETION DATE
2020

Opposite Southeast elevation.

Above Hawkins\Brown undertook a series of creative experiments and research into colour theory to design the patterns of colour that play across the towers' facades.

Hawkins\Brown's design proposals envisage generous roof terraces and high-level views of the two towers, looking across to the Queen Elizabeth Olympic Park.

Interior-design visualizations show the thoughtfully shared social spaces and ground-floor 'superlobby' that will form the heart of the new development.

Tideway will extend London's sewerage system to cope with the demands of the next century. It provides architects and artists with an unprecedented opportunity to enhance the appearance, identity and experience of one of the world's greatest cities through the creation of a series of new public spaces.

Of the twenty-four sites along the river, Hawkins\Brown have been awarded eight central locations, spanning five boroughs and stretching from Falconbrook Pumping Station in the west to Blackfriars Bridge in the east. Most are on the foreshore, above the civil engineering works, and each has the same aim: to bring people closer to the river.

A legacy to build on

For centuries the River Thames has been elemental to London's evolution, shaping its communities and driving its economy. Much of the capital's waste was dumped in the river, until, after the 'Great Stink' in the summer of 1858, Parliament allocated £3 million (about £340 million today) to the Metropolitan Board of Works to improve the city's polluted river.

Sir Joseph Bazalgette's design centred on the city's natural drainage system of 'lost rivers', such as the Fleet and the Effra, which flowed into his new interceptor sewers and then into sewage treatment works in east London. However, in times of severe storms, the system was designed to overflow through discharge points into the River Thames, rather than flood streets and homes. When Bazalgette's sewer system was completed, towards the end of the nineteenth century, this would have happened once or twice a year. Now that London's population has increased from two million to almost eight million people, it overflows every other week. In 2001 a multi-agency study was set up to assess the environmental impact. Following several years of investigation, the Tideway tunnel project was granted planning permission in 2014.

A grand scale

The tunnel generally follows the line of the Thames below ground, with vertical shafts projecting upwards at various points to capture flows and allow access. All sites require extensive coordination with subterranean engineering to ensure that the infrastructure can be maintained easily and efficiently.

The scope of the project is such that it has been granted a Development Consent Order (DCO). This kind of consent is for 'Nationally Significant Infrastructure Projects' and combines a grant of planning permission with a range of other separate consents, such as listed building consents and compulsory purchase orders. It's a hugely complex stakeholder arrangement that involves the Port of London Authority, the Environment Agency, Transport for London, the Marine Management Organisation, Historic England, Thames Water and the City of London, as well as local authorities and interest groups.

As part of the complex DCO planning consent, many sites have been approved based on indicative proposals, which means the architects must work within certain constraints. Hawkins\Brown are looking at eight sites, so they have developed a design framework that examines the cultural heritage of the Thames as a whole, as well as considering the local characteristics of each of the new destinations in order to reveal their unique identities and create opportunities for engagement and exploration.

Because many of the new destinations are influenced by their particular heritage and topography, it has been

Visualizations show how Hawkins\Brown are reimagining central London's largest open space at eight sites. Pictured here are Chelsea Embankment (opposite) and Blackfriars Bridge.

Tideway

River Thames

important to create a common thread across all eight sites. This is achieved through detailing in the signage and wayfinding, as well as Tideway's signature ventilation columns.

Art, heritage and landscape

In their designs, Hawkins\Brown were influenced by the project-wide Heritage Interpretation Strategy prepared in consultation with Historic England. The architects have also been involved in selecting the artists, who have been chosen carefully based on their understanding of the overarching spirit of the project's ambitions and the unique opportunities and constraints afforded by each location.

At Blackfriars Bridge, for example – the largest site, at more than 200 metres long – a new public space is being created for workers, tourists and passers-by to enjoy. The 'Fleet Path' design pays homage to the lost Fleet River, which originates on Hampstead Heath and flows down through the city before joining the Thames beneath Blackfriars Bridge. The landscaping is inspired by the lost river, recalling the flora and fauna of days gone by, while black stage sculptures by the artist Nathan Coley provide centres of gravity intended to engage and direct people across 4,000 square metres of new public realm.

At Albert Embankment, the design respects and enhances the sensitive riverside setting to create new public space on the foreshore. The site, in front of the infamous MI6 building at Vauxhall Cross, plays on its identity as a well-loved urban beach. The northern foreshore extends the Embankment and takes inspiration from the urban beach setting. The 'Isle of Effra' references the lost River Effra. This circular platform, which is framed with intertidal terraced planting on the southern foreshore, allows people to move further out on to the river. Plants were chosen that would have been found on the banks of the lost river.

At Chelsea Embankment, one of the illustrative concept sites under the DCO, Hawkins\Brown's design narrative responds to the restorative character of the local area, which is home to the Royal Hospital and one of the greenest areas of the city. Designed for moments of contemplation, the circular site appears as an extension of the river itself, its organic contours suggesting that it has been there for ever, eroded by the twice-daily ebb and flow of the water. The organic design uses clay bricks and intertidal planting, and features a floodable walkway that steps down, allowing people to get even closer to the river. By creating these distinct yet interconnected sites along the Thames, Hawkins\Brown are helping to put the river back at the heart of the city, and to bring people back to the river.

The proposed design of the new public space at Victoria Embankment, looking towards One Whitehall Place.

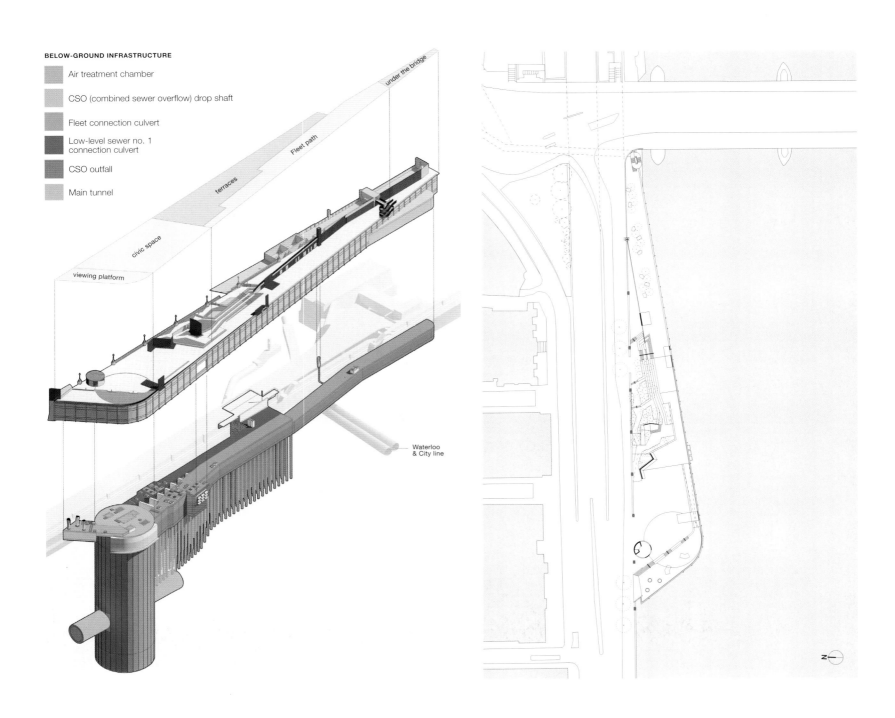

BELOW-GROUND INFRASTRUCTURE

- Air treatment chamber
- CSO (combined sewer overflow) drop shaft
- Fleet connection culvert
- Low-level sewer no. 1 connection culvert
- CSO outfall
- Main tunnel

under the bridge

Fleet path

terraces

civic space

viewing platform

Waterloo & City line

Above, left An exploded axonometric diagram illustrates the relationship between above-ground and underground works.

Above, right The site plan highlights Nathan Coley's sculptures.

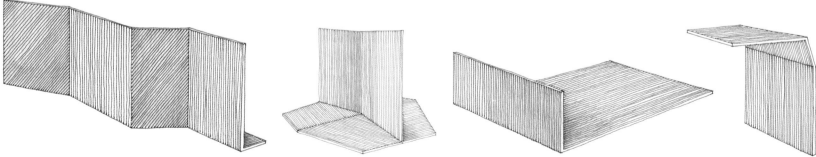

Top At the largest of the eight central sites, Hawkins\Brown worked with Nathan Coley on a series of black sculptures defining the various spaces along the foreshore, as shown in this aerial view of the proposed public realm.

Above Early conceptual sketches by the artist Nathan Coley.

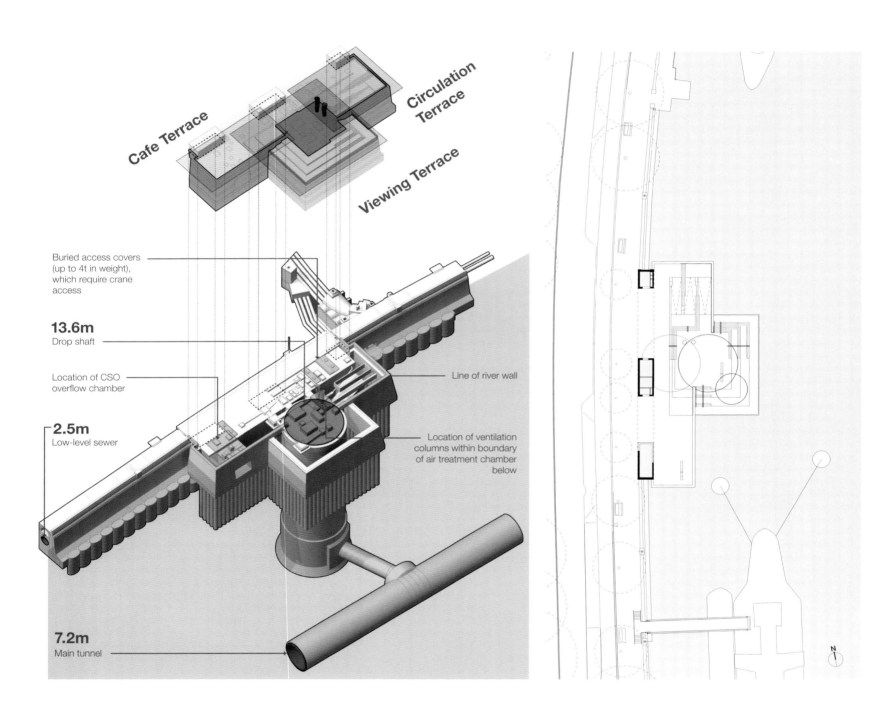

Cafe Terrace

Circulation Terrace

Viewing Terrace

Buried access covers (up to 4t in weight), which require crane access

13.6m
Drop shaft

Location of CSO overflow chamber

2.5m
Low-level sewer

Line of river wall

Location of ventilation columns within boundary of air treatment chamber below

7.2m
Main tunnel

Above, left An exploded axonometric diagram illustrates the relationship between above-ground and underground works.

Above Site plan.

A visualization of the proposed terrace and canopy structure, and a detail of Hawkins\Brown's conceptual model. The simple, elegant design of the new public space responds to the surrounding historic buildings and refers to the engineering structures hidden below the surface.

The design for this site extends the embankment to create an 'urban beach' that playfully reflects the tidal river and the Isle of Effra, marking the mouth of this lost river. Here the proposed space is seen from above during the day (right) and with the proposed night-time lighting.

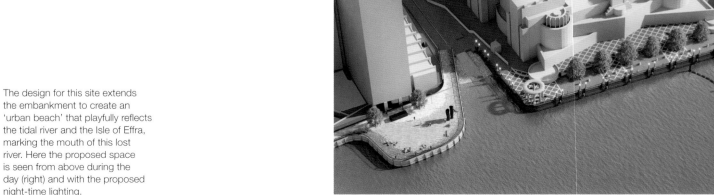

An early concept visualization
shows the Isle of Effra from
Vauxhall Bridge.

A conceptual model shows the
proposed terracing and planting.

Below Hawkins\Brown collaborated with the urban artist Florian Roithmayr, who extended the use of riverine materials to infuse the scheme with colour, enhancing the geometry of the site.

Bottom Early conceptual visualizations show the peaceful new space at high and low tide.

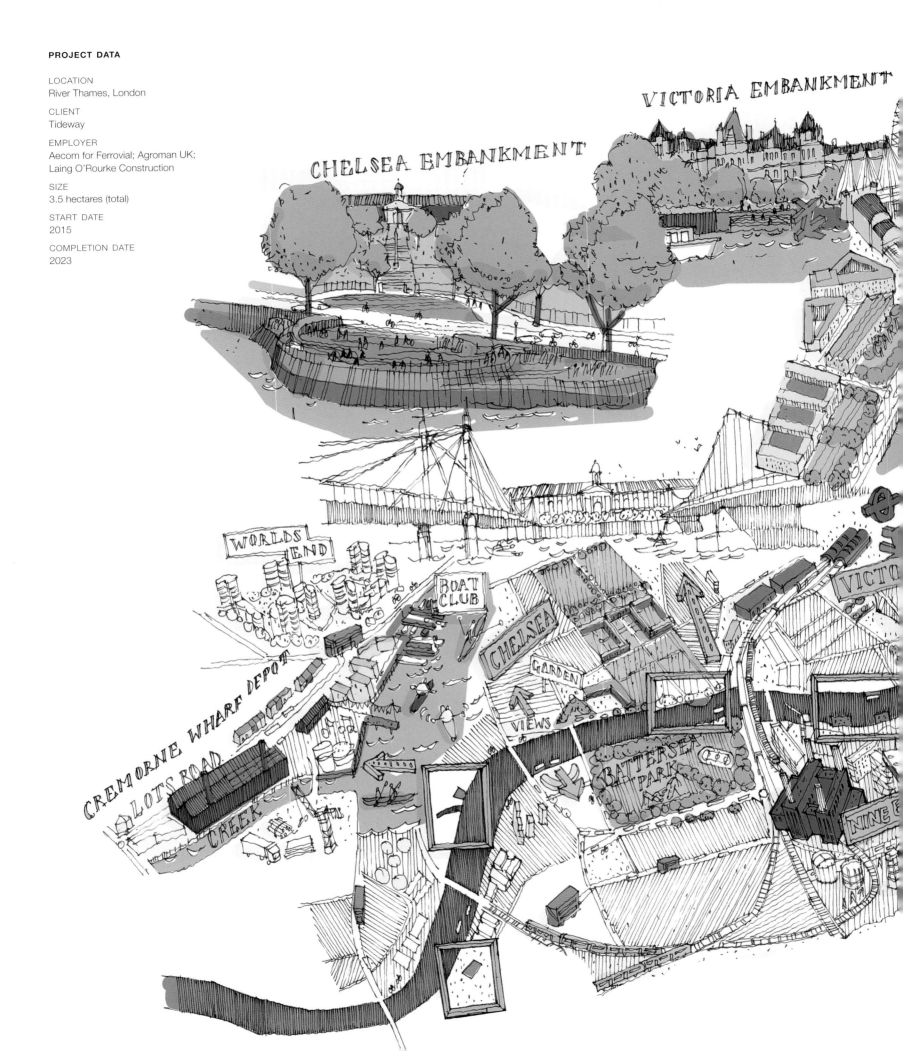

PROJECT DATA

LOCATION
River Thames, London

CLIENT
Tideway

EMPLOYER
Aecom for Ferrovial; Agroman UK;
Laing O'Rourke Construction

SIZE
3.5 hectares (total)

START DATE
2015

COMPLETION DATE
2023

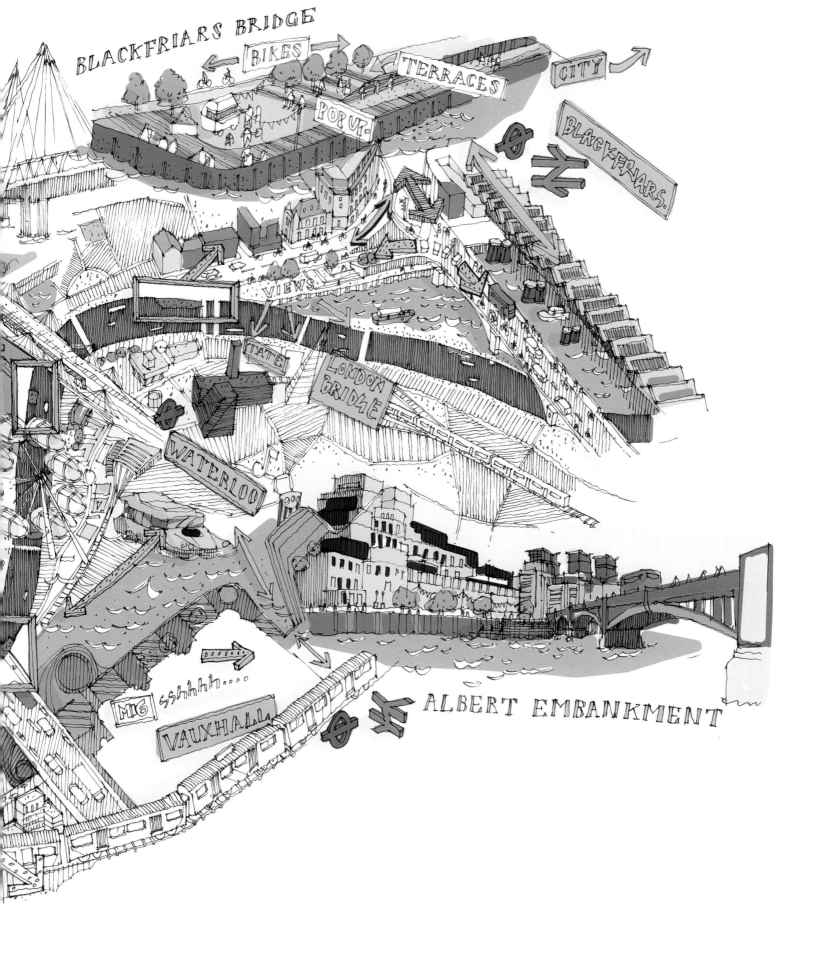

Oliver Milton and Jack Stewart

The power of data is a fairly recent revelation. Since about 2007 the automotive industry has gone through major change with the adoption of advanced 3D modelling processes and the streamlining of design through to manufacture. Today tech companies (among them Uber and Amazon) that use data to connect disparate elements of an industry are causing huge disruption and reaping the benefits. Change has taken longer in the construction industry, since there are more moving parts, but with recent increases in the abundance, accessibility and translatability of data, we are on the brink of a huge digital transformation across the industry.

The ramifications for architects and designers are huge. AutoCAD drawing software was released in 1982, and for about thirty years 2D and 3D CAD dominated. The software did not really innovate, however, being used alongside or in lieu of hand drawing, and the output was predominantly 2D printed drawings. Building Information Management (BIM) software is now the default, generating an abundance of building data ready for an explosion of briefing, building-in-use applications and coding interfaces. These are being built into our design software, enabling parametric, generative and algorithmic design and new machines that can turn this data into ready-assembled materials through digital fabrication. Waiting on the horizon are artificial intelligence, machine learning and robotics. It seems that designers are moving from 'point, click and draw' towards 'code and create', and data – the enabler – is at the centre.

The rate and breadth of change in the construction industry are unprecedented and reach far beyond the automated production of traditional design information. It's no wonder, then, that we, our collaborators, our clients and those who use the spaces we design are anxious about the rapid evolution of digital technology and data. But we should be excited, since we are already benefiting from the creativity and efficiency this new digital technology offers.

For many years old building projects have informed new ones, and so-called Post Occupancy Evaluation is now a requirement for many publicly procured buildings. But how much of this analysis is measurable and useful? How much time is spent going back and extracting the right information to allow comparison? Individual projects often have nuances that mean the lessons are hard to translate for new briefs.

At Hawkins\Brown we are seeing huge value in using the data completed projects generate to inform new briefs. We are developing in-house an online toolkit that will allow us to evaluate our past projects by extracting data directly from our BIM models. This will provide a precedent bank of schemes to enable benchmarking during the briefing process for new projects. By building on our experience we will ensure the goals of every building project are clear and informed from the outset, and the precedent bank will act as an intelligent, shared platform to track progress throughout design. Ultimately, this hard data store will help us to avoid what architects are so frequently criticized for: deviating from the brief.

The next step is to use the data that comes from a building to inform not how to design the next, but how to adapt or develop the completed building. WeWork, a co-working space provider, is doing just that, and to help the process it bought its own architecture studio in August 2015. The studio in question was CASE, described at the time by the architecture journalist Rory Stott as 'one of the leading voices in advocating technology in the architecture field'.

A move of this kind suggests a recognition that the provision of architectural services may not end once a building is complete, and that, to maximize the performance of workplaces for their tenants, the client may in fact need architects on hand and in-house at all times. They must be architects who understand the layers of interactive data their workplaces are continually producing, and who can use it to design systems or applications that respond to the needs of the users. In these examples, building data not only closes the loop between completion, use and briefing, but also makes design and delivery an evolving, cyclical process, where a final state is never reached. Constant redesign is encouraged as a response to rapidly changing conditions and requirements.

In 2018 architects are becoming modellers, coders, web designers and software engineers. At Hawkins\Brown, in just three years (2015–18) we moved from delivering only five projects in BIM to serving more than sixty live BIM projects. The main benefit of this software is the ability to append data to the geometries we are designing. Rather than using CAD to draw the components of a door as a set of lines, for example, we can now allocate data to a 3D component. The model knows that the door is a certain size, what ironmongery it is fitted with, its finish and colour, and so on. This information can be used to generate schedules of building components and data, to feed into cost and programme information and to inform a client of the door's technical requirements.

This is all now well understood by the industry. What is less familiar is the fact that the

Embracing Digital Transformation

process can work in the other direction, and the data can influence the geometries. This is an entirely new set of skills for architects to master: a new way of drawing, modelling or designing – through coding. Not only can we manipulate the data that constitutes our design, but also, through application-programming interfaces and built-in coding interfaces, we can manipulate the capability of the software. No longer are we at the mercy of the buttons provided by Autodesk and other software companies – we can build our own. Several projects in the studio have already benefited from this. Manual processes for which it would have taken an individual weeks to develop a single iteration become live using BIM. Rather than halting the design process, our design teams can now tweak the codes and watch 3D models update instantly.

One of our first forays into the potential of coding was for Here East (see pages 39–49). We developed a special 'dazzle-ometer' code that allowed us to generate unique glass frit patterns for the facade, while the solar control performance remained fixed. Once a pattern was chosen, the code was used to automate the setting out of every single constituent dot. Similarly, for the Life Sciences Building at the University of Sussex (due for completion in 2020), we built a code to set out a doubly curved wave of pendant light fittings. This enabled the designer to adjust the curvature of the light wave and the grid of pendants using a tangible set of control points, and to see the results instantly in 3D. More recently, we've been working on a facade colour pattern code dubbed the 'spandrel-izer'. This script was used for East Village (see pages 179–87), where it enabled the rapid testing of colour palettes and tints for more than 3,000 curtain-wall panels.

New ways of modelling and advances in manufacturing techniques are bringing designers closer to the fabrication and assembly of buildings. For Here East, this change has been particularly evident. A series of twenty-three artist studios will be built using the WikiHouse design and construction toolkit. This enables the creation of modular plywood buildings that are precision-manufactured using computer numerical control (CNC) milling machines. We collaborated with WikiHouse to develop a flexible design tool that would allow the user to alter the parameters of a building (roof type, footprint, height, door and window locations and sizes, and so on) and watch the 3D model regenerate itself live. The construction detail of the WikiHouse system was embedded into this software at concept design stage, and formed the production information that could be regenerated with each design change. Once the data is quality-checked we can send it – in the form of cutting files – directly to the CNC machine for fabrication.

This presents a huge opportunity. Machines will happily motor through repetitive tasks, once set up with the right instructions. They are becoming more sophisticated, and it is only a matter of time before the palette of materials, forms and systems becomes as diverse as designers and clients desire. Closing the gap between designer and builder provides architects with a reason and an opportunity to understand the details of the systems they are designing. A unique feature of Here East was that in this design-and-build project, it was the architect – rather than the contractor's specialist supply chain – that advised on the construction system.

It's exciting that architects can now evaluate the performance of their projects and keep track of progress in a much more definite and robust manner. The possibilities of continual assessment of and support for completed buildings, and the design of systems that can respond to evolving briefs, will extend the architect's role beyond soft landings (the transition from construction to occupation). The processes that are emerging enable architects to explore options more rapidly, ensure their designs are feasible and tackle ever more complex design challenges. They also allow designers to automate repetitive tasks or processes and remove the possibility of error.

It is evident that emerging technology is questioning the value of every role in the building process, from designer to bricklayer and all those in between. Agility is vital if all these contributors are to remain both competitive and relevant. At Hawkins\Brown we are working hard to ensure that we are at the cutting edge of what can be achieved. In everything we do, we strive to understand how technology can reinforce the human and social aspects of the design and construction processes, and translate those thoughts and explorations into the spaces we create. To do this we test and critique new technology, and – if it is valuable – look at how and where to implement it.

It is easy to jump to the conclusion that data-driven design results in standardization. But we are finding that data is enabling people to make better-informed decisions about design, to work in different ways and to remain in control of the design for longer. The manufacture of buildings is changing in a way that is opening up new possibilities, not closing them down. Design remains a human process; the new tools are just making it easier.

Acknowledgements

Contributor's Biography

Like any good architectural project, this book has come about only thanks to the talent and collaborative contributions of a huge cast of people. In particular, we would like to thank:

- Everyone at Hawkins\Brown who has worked so hard to produce this book: our essay contributors, the project teams who developed the building studies and especially the editorial team, who have agonized over every last detail: Seth Rutt, Hazel York, Shelley Smith and Alastair Roberts, ably supported by Gabriela Gmuzdek, Hattie Methven and Becci Price;
- The architects who produced the beautiful drawings that are central to the building studies: Keranie Theodosiou, From Works, Alex Dormon, Kane Carroll and, in particular, Jonathan Marsh;
- Hugh Pearman for his generous Introduction, Michael Evamy and Emma Hutton, who wrote the building studies, and the wide array of photographers and digital artists whose work illustrates this book so well;
- Nicola Bailey, Rosanna Fairhead and Hugh Merrell at Merrell Publishers, for their creative expertise, wisdom and patience.

We would also like to acknowledge the central role played by our clients, consultants, artists and many other collaborators whose support and ingenuity are evident throughout the projects illustrated in this book and across all the work we have done in our first thirty years as a practice.

At Hawkins\Brown, we understand that architecture is truly a team sport and that we would have achieved nothing without the critical input of all our partners, architects, interior and urban designers and support team, some of whom have been with us since the very beginning. Huge thanks to you all.

Roger Hawkins
Russell Brown

Hugh Pearman is an architecture critic, journalist and editor of the *RIBA Journal*, the magazine of the Royal Institute of British Architects. He lives in London.

Picture Credits

Index

First published 2018 by Merrell Publishers Limited,
London and New York

Merrell Publishers Limited
70 Cowcross Street
London EC1M 6EJ

merrellpublishers.com

British Library Cataloguing in Publication data:
A catalogue record for this book is available
from the British Library.

ISBN 978-1-8589-4668-9

Produced by Merrell Publishers Limited
Designed by Nicola Bailey
Edited by Rosanna Fairhead
Picture research by Nick Wheldon
Proofread by Marion Moisy
Indexed by Hilary Bird

Printed and bound in China

Front cover City of London Freemen's School
Swimming Pool, Ashtead, Surrey (pages 149–59)

Frontispiece Park Hill, Sheffield (pages 75–87)